MW00446711

MICROSOFT EXCEL 2016
IN *90* PAGES

by **Beth Brown**

Belleyre Books

Published by Belleyre Books
www.belleyrebooks.com
Delray Beach, FL

First Edition

ISBN 978-0-9986844-0-6 paperback
ISBN 978-0-9986844-1-3 eBook

Special discounts are available on quantity purchases by educational institutions, corporations, associations, and others. Please inquire at www.belleyrebooks.com/contact.

This text is in no way connected with Microsoft Corporation.

Microsoft and Microsoft Excel are either registered trademarks of the Microsoft Corporation in the United States and/or other countries. Screen shots and icons used with permission from Microsoft.

Names of all other products mentioned herein are used for identification purposes only and may be trademarks of their respective owners.

This book was created using Microsoft Word 2016.

Revision_1

Also in this Series

Microsoft Word 2016 in 90 pages

Microsoft PowerPoint 2016 in 90 pages coming soon!

Table of Contents

Tables

Preface

The goal of this book is to provide an approachable learning experience for Excel 2016. Through step-by-step directions, informative tables, and numerous screenshots, you'll be able to master Excel 2016 features to create professional, effective spreadsheets that store, organize, and analyze data.

Microsoft Excel 2016 in 90 Pages is written for Microsoft Excel 2016 that runs on Windows 10. However, if you have an earlier version of Windows, the differences will be minor as far as Excel 2016 is concerned.

How to Use this Book

Chapters divide the features of Excel into related topics with step-by-step instructions for each concept. You can apply these directions to a new spreadsheet or an existing one. References are made throughout the chapters to tables that further detail commands, actions, and features related to a concept.

Visit www.belleyrebooks.com for posts related to Microsoft Excel and this book and to print a shortcuts quick reference to Excel.

Accessibility Note

Keyboard shortcuts allow you to keep your hands on the keyboard for faster document development. Some keyboards shortcuts are faster and easier than trying to perform the same action with the mouse. In these cases, the keyboard shortcut is explicitly provided in the instructions.

Excel is an accessible application, and therefore, keyboard shortcuts are provided for essentially every possible command and action. You can determine these shortcuts by viewing the pop up ScreenTips (pg. 7) and by typing "keyboard shortcuts" into the Tell Me box (pg. 4). Further, pressing the Alt key once will display keyboard shortcuts for navigating the tabs and commands on the Ribbon.

About the Author

Beth Brown is the author of more than 40 computer science and computer applications textbooks. An engineering graduate of Florida Atlantic University, Ms. Brown holds a B.S. in Computer Science. She has worked with students and educators worldwide to develop Microsoft Office curriculum materials in addition to her work in programming, research and development, technical writing, and business.

Chapter 1
The Basics

Microsoft Excel 2016 is the ubiquitous spreadsheet application of the Microsoft Office 2016 productivity suite. Excel is used to organize data, analyze data through charts and tables, and create Data Models that use table relationships to analyze data. Learning Excel is essential to anyone who works in an office, goes to school, or uses a PC, laptop, tablet, or mobile phone to organize data.

Starting Excel

How you start Excel will depend on your device, but you will usually need to click the Excel 2016 icon in the Taskbar at the bottom of a PC screen or double-click the icon on the Desktop. If you don't see the Excel icon, click the Start menu in the lower-left corner of your screen and scroll through the list to locate the Excel 2016 icon (you may need to expand the Microsoft Office folder). Click this icon to start Excel.

The Excel Interface

The Excel *application interface* refers to the area where you interact with Excel. When you start Excel, the interface, also called the Excel window, displays the Start screen where you can choose to create a new file or open an existing file.

In the Start screen (Figure 1), click a link under Recent to open a file you've already created. If you want to create a new spreadsheet, click Blank workbook on the right side of the screen. A *workbook* is an Excel file. A new workbook contains a *worksheet*, or *sheet*, the Excel term for spreadsheet. You can add multiple sheets to the same workbook to keep related data together in one file.

The Excel window with a new workbook looks similar to Figure 2. Refer to Table 1 for information about the features.

Figure 1 The Start screen.

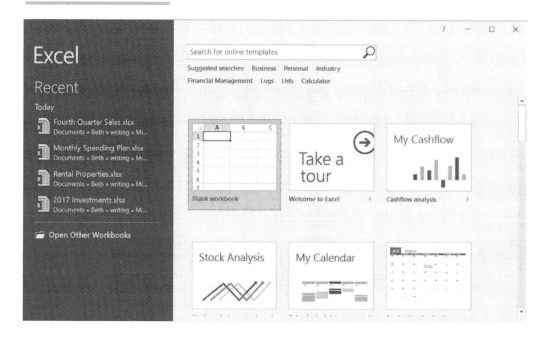

Figure 2 A new workbook.

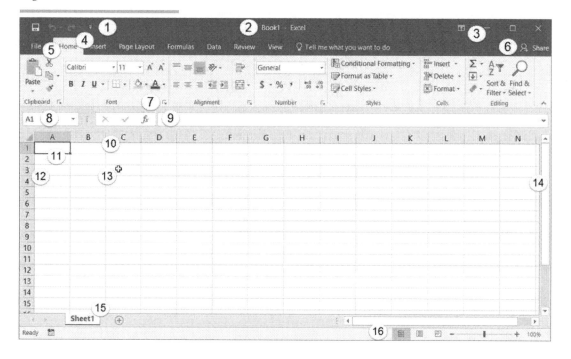

Table 1 The Excel Window

① Quick Access toolbar	Save, Undo, Redo
② File name	This is the name of your workbook. Book1 is the default name until you save your file with a more descriptive name.
③ Window controls	Minimize and Maximize window size. Close the window with the X button.
④ Ribbon	The Ribbon is divided into tabs that group commands (File, Home, Insert, Page Layout, Formulas, Data, Review, and View). Click the Ribbon Display Options button, near the window controls, to hide the Ribbon or reduce the Ribbon to tabs.
⑤ File tab	Displays the Backstage view where you can open, close, save as, print, and distribute your spreadsheet.
⑥ Share	Collaborate with others on a spreadsheet.
⑦ Dialog box launcher	Displays a dialog box with the options for a Ribbon group.
⑧ Name box	Displays the cell reference of the active cell. Type in the column letter and row number of a different cell and then press Enter to select that cell.
⑨ Formula bar	Displays the contents of the selected (active) cell. Click the insertion point in the Formula bar to edit cell contents.
⑩ Columns	Columns run vertically and are lettered from A to Z and then AA to XFD, up to 16,384 columns.

⑪ **Active cell**	A *cell* is the intersection of a row and column. The *active cell*, also called the *selected cell*, is indicated by a heavy border. Click a cell to make it active.
⑫ **Rows**	Rows run horizontally and are numbered 1 through 1,048,576.
⑬ **Cell pointer**	The white plus sign pointer is used to select cells on the spreadsheet.
⑭ **Scroll bars**	Used to bring unseen parts of your spreadsheet into view.
⑮ **Sheet tab**	Displays the name of the sheet in the workbook. Click ⊕ to add a new sheet to the workbook.
⑯ **Zoom controls**	The Status bar includes buttons for changing the way the spreadsheet is viewed. The Zoom controls and slider change the magnification.

TIP If the cell gridlines, Formula bar, or column and row headings are not displayed, click the View tab and select appropriate options from the Show group.

The Most Important Excel Feature

The Tell Me box is a feature new to Excel 2016 and is probably the most important Excel feature to know about. It is a powerful search and help tool that appears after the far right Ribbon tab. It's symbolized by a lightbulb with the text Tell me what you want to do (Figure 3).

Figure 3 The Tell Me box.

When you click Tell me what you want to do and then type a word or phrase, Excel suggests related commands (Figure 4).

Figure 4 Search text in the Tell Me box displays a menu of options.

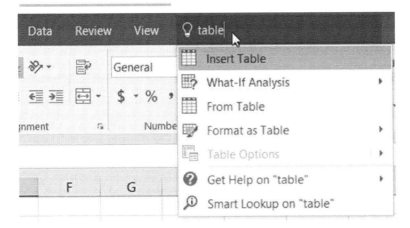

The Tell Me results menu is context sensitive. Different commands and actions will be displayed depending on what's going on in your spreadsheet.

At the bottom of the Tell Me results menu, there are options to display Help and perform a Smart Lookup. These commands display a *pane*, which is a set of options that remains open with your document. To close the pane, you click Close X in the upper-right corner.

The Tell Me box is the most important Excel feature because you no longer have to remember which Ribbon tab holds a command or which button is which — you can just get to work and ask Excel for whatever it is you need.

Communicating with Excel

Input devices are needed so that you can communicate with Excel. The devices you are most likely to use are the keyboard and mouse.

In an Excel spreadsheet, the data you type on the keyboard is entered into the *active cell*, which is indicated by a heavy border. The name of the active cell is displayed in the Name box. Refer to Figure 5.

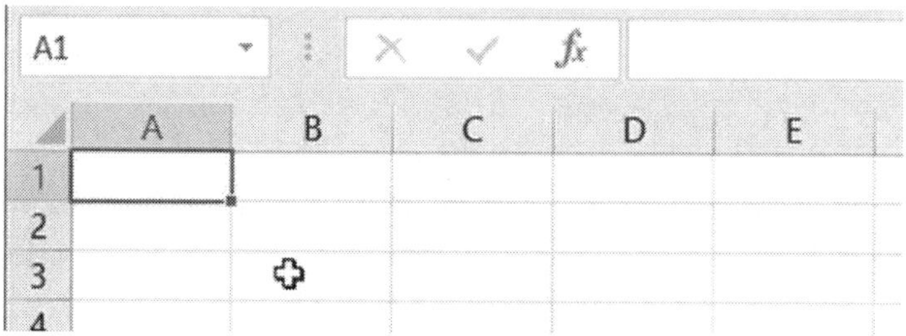

Figure 5 Cell A1, with the heavy border, is the active cell.

Special keys on the keyboard are used to select a cell to make it active, while the Escape key allows you to cancel an action, such as the display of a dialog box. The Ctrl key is used in combination with other keys to perform an action. Refer to Table 2.

Table 2 Keyboard Keys and their Functions

 Esc	Press the Escape (Esc) key to cancel the current action, including data entry.
 Ctrl	The Control (Ctrl) key is used in combination with other keys. You must press and hold the Ctrl key before pressing a second key. For example, Ctrl+S means to press and hold Ctrl while pressing the S key once.
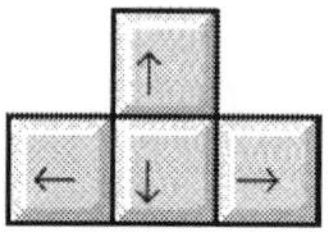 ↑ ← ↓ →	Press an arrow key to select a cell in that direction. Press Ctrl+arrow key to select the first or last cell in that direction.
 Tab	Press Tab to select the next cell in a row. Press Shift+Tab to select the previous cell in a row.
 Enter	Press Enter to select the next cell in a column. Press Shift+Enter to select the previous cell in a column.
 Home	Press Home to select the first cell in the current row. Ctrl+Home selects the cell A1.

End	Press End to select the last used cell in a row. Ctrl+End selects the bottom-right used cell of a spreadsheet. End, arrow key selects the last used cell in the direction of the arrow.
Page Up Page Down	The Page Up (PgUp) and Page Down (PgDn) keys are used to scroll a worksheet.
Delete	Press the Delete key to remove the selected cell's contents.
← Backspace	The Backspace key removes the selected cell's contents and displays the I-Beam pointer in the cell.

The mouse is a pointing device that displays a graphic image called a *pointer*. You can use the mouse to select commands on the Ribbon, respond to prompts, select cells, and position the text insertion point for editing cell contents. When you rest (hover) the mouse pointer on a command or feature of the interface a helpful *ScreenTip* pops up, as shown in Figure 6.

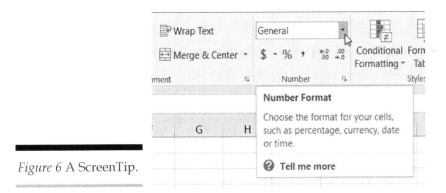

Figure 6 A ScreenTip.

The pointer shape changes depending on where the pointer is placed. One exception is when Excel is working on an action, which is indicated by an hourglass pointer. You can further communicate with Excel with different actions through the mouse buttons. Refer to Table 3.

Table 3 Mouse Actions and Pointer Shapes

Point	Move the mouse until the pointer is placed on a cell, an object, or in a specific area.
Click	Press and release the left mouse button once.
Double-click	Press and release the left mouse button twice in rapid succession.
Right-click	Press and release the right mouse button once.
Drag	Press and hold the left mouse button while moving the mouse. This action selects multiple cells together or positions a graphic object.
Scroll wheel	If available, rotate the scroll wheel to move a spreadsheet up or down to bring unseen parts into view.
↖	The arrow pointer is displayed when the mouse pointer is positioned over a command or another clickable object.
✛	The white cross pointer is displayed when the mouse pointer is positioned over a cell. Click to select the cell.
I	The I-beam pointer is displayed when the mouse pointer is in an area where text can be typed. Click the I-beam to place the insertion point.
👆	The hand shape is typical when the mouse pointer is positioned over a hyperlink. Click to follow a link.

The Backstage View

The File tab on the Excel Ribbon displays a screen called the *Backstage view*. From here, you work with files, print, and set Excel options, among other things. You can click ⊕ at any time when you want to return to your document. Click a command on the left side of the Backstage view screen to display related options:

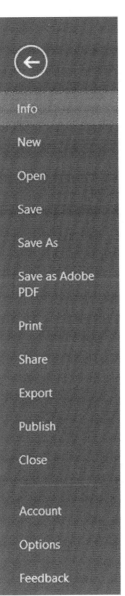

Info displays the properties and other information about your document. Chapter 7 discusses the Document Inspector.

New displays the Start screen, including templates which are discussed further in Chapters 2 and 7.

Open displays links to recently opened files. Click Browse to display the Open dialog box where you can navigate to other files.

Save As is used to save a worksheet with a new name. If you want to save the copy in a new location, click Browse and then navigate to the desired folder in the Save As dialog box. You also have the option of changing the file format to PDF or any one of a number of file types when you click the Save as type list below the File name box.

Print displays a print preview with options for selecting your printer and changing print settings, which include printing the active sheet, an entire workbook, or just a selected area of a sheet, margins options, and scaling options for fitting a spreadsheet onto a sheet of paper.

Share displays options for emailing your spreadsheet or making it available to others for editing or viewing. Click Email to send your document as an Excel attachment or as a PDF attachment (the recommended method to preserve formatting and prevent changes to your spreadsheet). Refer also to Chapter 7.

Export has options for creating a PDF. There are also options for converting a spreadsheet file to a different file type. For example, you may need a CSV (comma delimited) text file with no formatting. When a file is exported, the original remains and a new file is created.

Publish allows you to export your workbook to Microsoft Power BI for creating interactive reports and dashboards.

Close removes your workbook from the Excel window without closing Excel.

Account displays information about your version of Excel.

Options displays the Excel Options dialog box for customizing how Excel interacts with you. With this dialog box you can access options related to formula calculation and error handling, auto save, AutoCorrect, the Ribbon, and the Quick Access toolbar.

The Backstage view doesn't include a quit command. If you are ready to quit Excel and close the application interface, click Close X in the upper-right corner of the Excel window. If you've made unsaved changes to an open spreadsheet, you will be prompted to either save or discard the changes before quitting.

The Save command deserves special attention. Because you want to be executing this command often — every minute of two if you're doing a lot of data entry and editing — Excel provides several ways to save a file:

- The Save command on the File tab. However, this is a rather weighty way to have to get to a command you want to execute often.

- The Save button on the Quick Access toolbar.

- And if you want to keep your hands on the keyboard, press Ctrl+S to save your document (press and hold the Ctrl key and then press the S key once).

Chapter 2
Creating a New Spreadsheet

Creating a new spreadsheet involves starting Excel, choosing a spreadsheet template, and then entering and organizing your data.

First Things First

Planning a Spreadsheet

A screen full of blank cells can be intimidating. It might even tempt you to start entering data at random. Don't waste your time. Always plan your spreadsheet before attempting to create one in Excel. Without a plan, you may end up with a jumble of data that has little chance of being useful for analysis.

The steps for planning a spreadsheet are:

1. **Determine what information the spreadsheet is to produce. In other words, what questions should it answer?**
2. **Determine the data needed by the spreadsheet. (This will usually depend on step 1.)**
3. **Decide how to organize the data.**

Spreadsheets are used to answer questions such as what are the total sales, how many items do we need to sell to make a profit, what are my spending requirements for August. Determining the information your spreadsheet is to produce will help you focus on the related data you need to store in the spreadsheet.

The structure of a spreadsheet is based on rows and columns. Columns logically group data, while rows are used to present singular items. For example, a spending plan should list expense items in rows with columns grouping the expenses per month.

Choosing a Spreadsheet Template

Whether you're at the Excel Start screen or the File ⇨ New screen, you'll need to decide which template you want to use for your new spreadsheet. A *template* is a file that already has some formatting and, in some cases, formulas for doing calculations. When you create a new spreadsheet, you are using a supplied Excel template. Excel Blank workbook is the most basic template, displaying a workbook with one empty sheet and no cell formatting. Other templates will make more sense after you've learned more about Excel.

Entering Data

Data includes numeric values, dates, times, and text. An effective spreadsheet will also include *labels* that title the worksheet and describe the data in the rows and columns, as in Figure 7.

◢	A	B	C	D	E
1	**Next Level Tacos Food Truck**				
2					
3	**Payroll**	4/7/2017			
4					
5	**Employee**	**Position**	**Hourly Rate**	**Hours**	**Pay**
6	Berke	Assembler	$10.25	25	$256.25
7	Nguyen	Chef	$15.00	30	$450.00
8	Rodriguez	Chef	$15.00	28	$420.00
9	Wilson	Cashier	$11.50	30	$345.00
10					

Figure 7 This spreadsheet has labels in rows 1 and 5. Data is stored in rows 6 through 10.

Numeric data is automatically right aligned in a cell, and text is left aligned. Changing alignment for better readability is covered in Chapter 3.

To enter data and labels into a spreadsheet:

1. Click a cell to make it the active cell (Table 4 lists other methods for selecting cells). The cell displays a solid border.

2. Type the label or data for the cell. As you type, the entry is also displayed on the Formula bar.

3. Press Enter to enter the label or data. The next cell in the column is selected.

Or

Press Tab to enter the label or data. The next cell in the row is selected.

Or

Click ✔ on the Formula bar to enter the label or data. The same cell remains selected.

Or

Click ✕ on the Formula bar or press the Esc key to cancel the entry.

4. Repeat steps 2 and 3 to enter the remaining labels and data for the worksheet, being sure that you first select the appropriate cell for your data.

TIP The fastest way to enter data is row by row, using the Tab and Enter keys to select cells. With this approach, you begin by selecting the cell in the upper-left of the spreadsheet, type the value for that cell, press the Tab key to move to the next cell in the row, type the value for that cell, and so on, until the first row is complete. After typing the last entry for the row, press Enter, rather than Tab, which automatically selects the first cell in the next row.

TIP To break data over two lines within a cell, press Ctrl+Enter at the end of the first line.

Changing Column Widths

Text and labels that extend beyond the width of a column will appear to flow into the adjoining empty cell(s), but the data is actually only stored in the first cell. When adjoining cells also contain data, long text and labels will be truncated to the width of the column they are stored in (as with cell A4 in Figure 8). Numeric data that is too large for a cell may be displayed as #####. To widen a cell, you must change the entire column's width.

Figure 8 Columns A and E need to be wider to display their contents entirely.

A4		✕ ✓ *fx*	Berkshire Hathaway	
	A	B	C	D	E
3	Company	Ticker	Current Price	Shares	Value
4	Berkshire	BRK.A	$244,590.01	5	##########

To change column width:

1. Point to the right boundary of the column to resize. The pointer changes to a double-headed arrow shape (Figure 9).

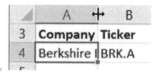

Figure 9 Drag or double-click the column boundary to size a column.

2. Double-click the column boundary for an autofit. This best fit method automatically sizes the column to the width of its widest entry.

Or

Drag the column boundary to the desired width.

Or

Right-click a column letter. A menu is displayed. Click Column Width, type a value in the displayed dialog box, and then click OK.

TIP The value associated with a column width or row height roughly equates to the number of characters that can be displayed. The default width of 8.43 displays about 8 characters in a cell, while the default height of 12.75 displays characters of about 11 points.

TIP Drag or double-click a row boundary to change row height.

TIP Click Home ⇨ Format for additional commands that change column widths and row heights.

TIP To improve spreadsheet readability, double-click or drag a column border to decrease column width when data is much shorter than the current width.

Ensuring Accurate Data

The reliability of a spreadsheet and the data it produces is based on the accuracy of the data entered. Excel has several features for improving data accuracy.

The *AutoCorrect* feature compares the characters you type to a list and then automatically makes changes when there is a match. For example, when you type adn, it is converted to "and"; ahve is converted to "have". AutoCorrect also converts specified character sequences to special characters. For example, when you type (c) in a cell it is converted to ©. Similarly, (r) is changed to ® and (tm) is changed to ™. To reverse an AutoCorrect action, press Ctrl+Z immediately after it happens.

To view the AutoCorrect list and edit entries:

1. Click File ⇨ Options ⇨ Proofing ⇨ AutoCorrect Options. The dialog box displays a scrollable AutoCorrect list.

2. To add a new entry, type the appropriate text in the Replace and With boxes and then click Add.

3. To remove an existing entry, click the entry in the list and then click Delete.

TIP To make data entry faster, add acronyms for your company name and other frequently typed phrases to the AutoCorrect list. When you type an acronym, it will be replaced by the complete phrase you entered.

The *AutoComplete* feature considers the data in the cells above the selected cell to suggest an entry (numbers, dates, and times are not considered). When the first few characters of the entry you are typing matches an entry above, AutoComplete suggests an entry, highlighting the additional text, as in Figure 10.

	A	B	C
1	**Vendor**	**Item**	**Quantity**
2	City Produce	lettuce	12
3	Aztec Shells	tortillas	250
4	City Produce		

Figure 10 AutoComplete compares what you are typing to column entries above.

You have three options when AutoComplete recognizes an entry:

- Press Enter to accept the entry and select the next cell in the column.

- Continue typing to overwrite the characters suggested by AutoComplete.

- Press Backspace to remove the suggested characters. For example, to enter just "City" in cell A4 of Figure 10, type City and then press Backspace to remove additional characters before pressing Enter to accept the entry.

TIP To disable AutoCorrect, click File ⇨ Options ⇨ Advanced and then clear the Enable AutoComplete for cell values checkbox.

The last feature to improve data accuracy is the *spelling checker*.

To check the spelling of text in a spreadsheet:

1. Click Review ⇨ Spelling. (Or press F7.) A dialog box is displayed.

2. If Excel comes across a cell with text that is not in its dictionary file, then the dialog box has spelling options.

   a) Click Ignore Once or Ignore All if the word is correct as is.

      Or

      Click Add to Dictionary to prevent the spelling checker from flagging the word in the future.

      Or

      Click a correctly spelled word in the Suggestions box and then click Change or Change All.

      Or

      Click a correctly spelled word in the Suggestions box and then click AutoCorrect to have the misspelled word and the correctly spelled word added to the AutoCorrect list.

3. When there are no unrecognized words in your spreadsheet, or after spell check is complete, a dialog box informs you that you are good to go.

TIP Click Review ⇨ Thesaurus when you want to replace a word with a synonym that is similar in meaning.

TIP Press Shift+F5 to display a dialog box for finding and replacing text. Click Home ⇨ Find & Select for additional options.

Inserting Special Characters

When your data includes a character or symbol that isn't on the keyboard, such as á or ¢, you use Insert ⇨ Symbols ⇨ Symbol (Figure 11). The command displays a dialog box with symbols and special characters.

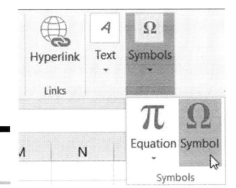

Figure 11 The Symbol command.

Hyperlink Data

Inserting an active link into a cell is as easy as typing it. Excel interprets text such as @, .com, and www. as part of a hyperlink and automatically converts the text into a link. If you distribute the file as an Excel spreadsheet or as a PDF, the viewer will be able to click links in the document to follow them.

To reverse an unwanted conversion, click Undo on the Quick Access toolbar (Ctrl+Z) immediately after entering data, or right-click the link and select Remove Hyperlink. To convert text that wasn't automatically converted, right-click and select Hyperlink to display a dialog box where you specify Link to, Text to display, and Address information.

Editing Cell Data

If a cell contains a complicated formula or long text entry, it may be easier to *edit* the contents of the cell, rather than retype the entire entry.

To edit existing cell contents:

> 1. Select the cell with the contents to edit.

2.   Point to the Formula bar and then click the I-beam pointer to place the insertion point.

Or

Double-click the cell with the contents to edit. The cell displays an I-beam pointer.

3.   Press the right and left arrow keys to move the insertion point as needed.

4.   Press Delete to remove characters to the right of the insertion point.

Or

Type text to add to the entry.

5.   Press Enter to update the entry after edits are complete.

TIP When text is selected with the mouse, a mini toolbar appears with formatting options. The mini toolbar is discussed in Chapter 3.

Organizing a Worksheet

As your spreadsheet evolves, you may find that data needs to be reorganized. Cells might need to be moved, duplicated, or deleted, or you may need to insert, delete, or transpose rows and columns. The commands used in the steps below are summarized in Table 5.

To delete, duplicate, move, or insert cells:

1.   Select the cell to move, duplicate, or delete.

Or

Select a range of cells to move, duplicate, or delete.

Selecting a range of cells is the process of dragging the mouse pointer from one cell to another, highlighting the range, as in Figure 12. (Refer to Table 4 for other methods to select multiple cells.) If you need to clear the selection, click anywhere outside the highlighted cells.

Figure 12 The selected cell range A3:D4.

	A	B	C	D
1	**Ad Campaign**	**Impressions**	**Clicks**	**Sales**
2	College Target	10,734	70	$430.00
3	Word Hook	14,050	200	$650.00
4	Brand Awareness	7,435	45	$390.00

A range is indicated with a colon (:) between the first and last cell names.

2. If you want to **delete** the contents of a selected cell or cell range, press the Delete key.

Or

Right-click the selected cell or cell range and click Clear Contents.

3. If you want to **remove** the selected cell or cell range from the worksheet and shift surrounding cells into the vacated location, click Home ⇨ Delete. To specify how surrounding cells are shifted into the vacated location, click Home ⇨ Delete ⇨ Delete Cells instead.

Or

Right-click the selected cell or cell range and click Delete. Cells are automatically shifted.

4. If you want to **duplicate** the selected cell or cell range, click Home ⇨ Copy. The selection displays a moving border. Next, click the destination cell and then click Home ⇨ Paste. (If you selected a range, the upper-left corner of the range will be pasted starting at the selected destination.) Press Esc to remove the moving border.

5. If you want to **move** the selected cell or cell range, click Home ⇨ Cut. The selection displays a moving border. Next, click the destination cell and then click Home ⇨ Paste. (If you selected a range, the upper-left corner of the range will be pasted starting at the selected destination.)

Or

Point to the heavy border around the selection until the pointer changes to the four-headed arrow move pointer, as shown in Figure 13. Drag the border with the move pointer to move the selection to a new location.

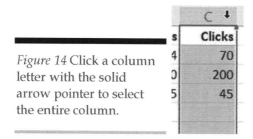

Figure 13 Drag a range with the move pointer to move it to a new location.

6. If you want to **insert** cells, select the cell where you want to insert a blank cell or select the range where you want a range of blank cells. Next, click Home ⇨ Insert. To specify how the selected cell and surrounding cells are shifted to make room for the new cells, click Home ⇨ Insert ⇨ Insert Cells instead.

    Or

    Right-click the selected cell or cell range and click Insert. You will be prompted to select how cells are shifted.

To insert, delete, move, and transpose rows and columns:

1. If you want to **delete a column**, right-click the column letter and click Delete.

    Or

    Click the column letter to select the entire column (Figure 14) and then click Home ⇨ Delete.

Figure 14 Click a column letter with the solid arrow pointer to select the entire column.

C
Clicks
70
200
45

2. If you want to **delete a row**, right-click the row number and click Delete.

    Or

    Click the row number to select the entire row and then click Home ⇨ Delete.

3. If you want to **insert a column or row**, right-click the column letter or row number and click Insert.

    Or

    Click the column letter or row number to select it and then click Home ⇨ Insert.

4. If you want to **move a column**, select it and then click Home ⇨ Cut. Next, select the column at the destination position and click Home ⇨ Insert. Similarly, use Cut and Insert to move selected rows.

5. If you find that your data would be better represented by rotating the rows and columns, you can transpose the data onto a different section of the spreadsheet and then delete the original data.

     To **transpose** a selected range of data, click Home ⇨ Copy, right-click the first cell where you want the transposed data to appear, and then click the Transpose button under Paste Options in the displayed menu. Note that you must Copy the cells rather than Cut for the Transpose button to be available.

TIP Multiple rows and columns can be inserted or deleted at once by first selecting them together before clicking Insert or Delete.

TIP To divide text from one column into multiple columns, insert the appropriate number of columns to the right of the column you are separating and then click Data ⇨ Text to Columns for the three-step Text to Columns Wizard.

Table 4 Selecting Cells and Ranges

Range selection using the mouse	Click the first cell in a range and then drag the mouse pointer to the last cell in the range.
Range selection using the F8 key	Select the first cell in a range, press F8, and then use the arrow keys to move to the last cell in the range. Press F8 again to end selection.
Range selection using the Shift key	Select the first cell in the range and then press and hold the Shift key while you click the last cell in the range. This is useful for a large range selection that requires scrolling to bring the last cell of the range into view.

Range selection using the Name box	Select the first cell in the range, click in the Name box and type the cell name for the last cell in the range, and then press and hold Shift when you press Enter.
Column, Row selection	Click the column letter or row number. Drag across column or row headings to select multiple columns or rows, or select the first column or row and then press and hold the Shift key while clicking the last column or row for the selection.
Spreadsheet region with data	Select the cell in the upper-left of a spreadsheet and then press Ctrl+Shift+End.
Ctrl+A	Press Ctrl+A to select the region of cells with data. Press Ctrl+A a second time to select the entire worksheet.
Ctrl	Use the Ctrl key to select nonadjacent cells: Select a cell, range, column, or row, and then press and hold Ctrl while clicking or selecting other cells, ranges, columns, or rows.

The tools for organizing a spreadsheet are in the upper-left of the Excel window, in the Quick Access toolbar, and on the Home tab, as shown in Figure 15. The Cut and Copy commands place selected cell contents onto the *Clipboard*, a storage area in memory, for use later. Refer to Table 5.

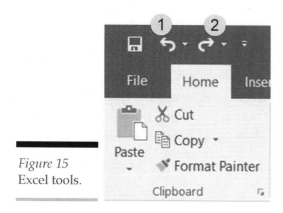

Figure 15
Excel tools.

Table 5 Tools for Organizing a Spreadsheet

① Undo	Reverses the most recent action. Click the Undo arrow to choose from a list of actions to reverse.
② Repeat Typing	Reverses the last Undo.
Home ➪ Cut	Click Cut (Ctrl+X) to remove selected cell contents and place it on the Clipboard.
Home ➪ Copy	Click Copy (Ctrl+C) to place a duplicate of selected cell contents onto the Clipboard, leaving the original data unchanged.
Home ➪ Paste (Ctrl) ▾	Click Paste (Ctrl+V) to insert the last cut or copied cell contents into the selected cell. Click the Paste arrow for paste options, or, after pasting, click the Paste Options button to control how the data is pasted. Refer also to Table 10 on pg. 50.
Home ➪ Clipboard dialog box launcher	Click the dialog box launcher in the lower-right corner of the Clipboard group to open the Clipboard task pane. Click an item on the Clipboard to place it in the selected cell.
Home ➪ Delete	Deletes selected cells, rows, or columns.
Home ➪ Insert	Inserts cells, rows, or columns.
	Select a cell or range and then point to the heavy border until the pointer changes to the move pointer. Drag the cell or range border with the move pointer to move it to a new location.
←Backspace	Press to remove a character to the left of the insertion point when editing cell data.
Delete	Press to remove the contents of a selected cell. Press to remove a character to the right of the insertion point when editing cell data.

Filling a Series

Worksheet development often involves extending, copying, or completing a series based on the current data. For this, Excel displays an *Auto Fill Options* button when you drag the *Fill handle* (Figure 16). The fill handle is discussed again in Chapter 4 on pg. 51.

Figure 16 The fill handle was dragged from A1 to E1 to complete a series. The Auto Fill Options button was clicked to specify how to complete the selection.

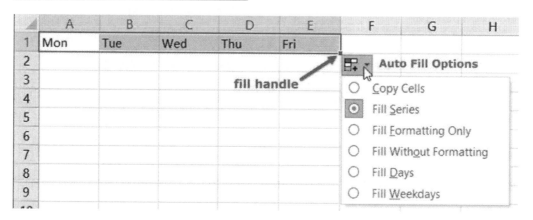

To enter data using the fill handle:

1. Enter data for at least the first item in a series. Excel recognizes dates, days of the week, times, and numbers. If you want a pattern to be filled, for example, 1, 3, 5…, then enter enough data for Excel to identify the series.

2. Select the first cell of the series or enough cells to provide the series pattern. Refer to Figure 17.

Figure 17 To fill a series, select enough cells to define the pattern.

3. Drag the fill handle to the cells you want to fill. (The pointer changes to a solid cross when you point to the fill handle.)

4. If necessary, click Auto Fill Options (shown in Figure 16) for additional fill options.

TIP You can also click Home ⇨ Fill to complete a series.

TIP To disable the fill handle, click File ⇨ Options ⇨ Advanced and then clear the Enable fill handle and cell drag-and-drop checkbox.

Using Multiple Sheets

As a workbook develops, you will most likely need additional spreadsheets in your workbook for charts, related data, and reports. A well-organized workbook will be easier to use and comprehend.

To manage sheets:

1. To add a sheet, click ⊕ to the right of the last sheet tab.

    Or

    Click Home ⇨ Insert ⇨ Insert Sheet.

2. To move or copy a sheet, right-click the sheet tab and click Move or Copy. A dialog box is displayed.

    a) If there is more than one spreadsheet file open, you can choose to move or copy the sheet to another workbook. Click the To book list arrow and select the appropriate workbook, if necessary.

    b) In the Before sheet list, click the position for the sheet.

    c) If you want to duplicate the sheet, click the Create a copy checkbox.

    d) Select OK.

3. To remove a sheet and all its data, right-click the sheet tab and click Delete.

TIP Additional sheet tab commands are discussed in the chapters following.

The Zoom Controls

Entering data for your spreadsheet can be easier with a close-up view. Use the Zoom controls in the lower-right of the Excel window to change the magnification of your spreadsheet. Click + to increase the magnification, click – to reduce; or drag the slider in either direction. Click 100% to display the Zoom dialog box. Note that 100% displays data close to actual size; however, the magnification does not affect the size of the text when printed.

Zoom commands on the View tab include Zoom to Selection for quickly magnifying an area. Click 100% to return to the default view.

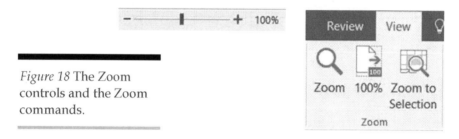

Figure 18 The Zoom controls and the Zoom commands.

Chapter 3
Formatting and Sorting

Spreadsheet formatting is important because it impacts the reader's ability to understand the data in many ways. Eye-catching bold labels distinguish data areas, while a logo image provides brand recognition. Conditional formats allow a reader to immediately evaluate related data. If you will be providing the spreadsheet to others for data entry, then color coded cells provide a better user interface. Sorting analyzes data through organization.

Fonts and Borders

Font refers to the shape, style, and size of characters. The default font in Excel is Calibri. A similar font is Arial. These fonts display clear, readable numbers and text. Applying styles such as **bold** and *italic* to labels can further improve comprehension, and a larger font size makes information easier to read. Where needed, you can format individual characters, such as in a label that includes a subscript.

The Home ⇨ Borders command (Figure 20) has options including All Borders and Thick Outside Borders. Formatting a spreadsheet with borders makes a printout easier to read. Selecting a range of cells and formatting it with a thick outside border is a way to segment related data.

TIP Carefully choose styles. Underline can be confused with a link, and numbers formatted in red can be misinterpreted as negative numbers.

To format cells:

1. Select the cell(s) to format.
2. Click commands in the Font group on the Home tab (Figure 19).

   Or

   Click the Font dialog box launcher in the Font group on the Home tab and then set options on the Font and Border tabs.

To format characters within a cell:

1. Double-click the cell with the contents to format. The cell displays the I-beam pointer.
2. Select the individual character(s) to format.

3.   Click commands in the Font group on the Home tab (Figure 19).

Or

Click commands on the mini toolbar (available when you use the mouse to select characters in a cell).

Or

Click the Font dialog box launcher in the Font group on the Home tab and then set options on the Font tab.

The mini toolbar options (Figure 21) are limited compared to the Font group (Figure 19) and the Font dialog box.

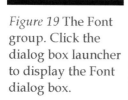

Figure 19 The Font group. Click the dialog box launcher to display the Font dialog box.

Click a command arrow for a menu of choices. For example, the Borders command has several options (Figure 20).

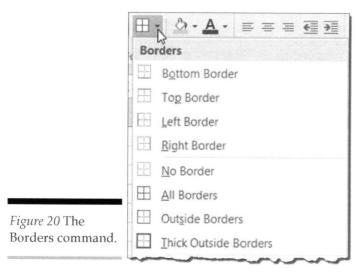

Figure 20 The Borders command.

Figure 21 The mini toolbar is displayed when you select text with the mouse.

TIP To remove all formats from selected cells, click Home ⇨ Clear.

Alignment and Merging Cells

Alignment refers to the position of content within a cell. By default, labels are left aligned and numbers, dates, and times are right aligned. A good practice is to format column labels with the same alignment as their corresponding data. For example, the month labels in Figure 22 are right aligned to match their numeric data. Alignment options include left, right, center, top, middle, bottom, angled, vertical, rotated, and indented. Click Increase Indent ➤≣ when you want to indent data because spaces affect calculations and sorting.

When you have a label that titles two or more columns of data, you can merge and center the label above the columns to provide a better layout (A1:G2, A3:A4, B3:B4, and C3:G3 are merged in Figure 22). Merged cells contain the content from the upper-left cell of the range. You can also wrap text within a cell or merged range (cell B3 in Figure 22).

To align cell content:

1. Select the cell(s) to format.

2. Click commands in the Alignment group on the Home tab. If rotating text, click the Orientation arrow to display options.

To merge and center cells:

1. Select the cells to merge.

2. Click Home ⇨ Merge & Center.

TIP For other merge options, click the Home ⇨ Merge & Center arrow. To split merged cells, click Home ⇨ Merge & Center again.

▬▬▬▬▬▬▬▬▬▬

Figure 22 Merged, aligned, and formatted cells.

	Stock	Ticker Symbol	End of Month Close Price				
			Jan	Apr	Jul	Oct	Dec
Portfolio 2016							
Amazon	AMZN		$587.00	$659.59	$758.81	$789.82	$749.87
Microsoft	MSFT		$55.09	$49.87	$56.68	$59.92	$62.14
Google	GOOG		$742.95	$693.01	$768.79	$784.54	$771.82

Number Formats

Formatting numeric data conveys the meaning of a value. The Number Format list (Figure 23) provides a default format for many types of data. Additional formats can be selected by clicking the Number Format dialog box launcher in the Number group on the Home tab. Note that applying a format does not change the stored value, only the way it is displayed.

To format numeric data:

1. Select the cell(s) to format.
2. Click the Number Format arrow in the Number group on the Home tab and then click an option (Figure 23).

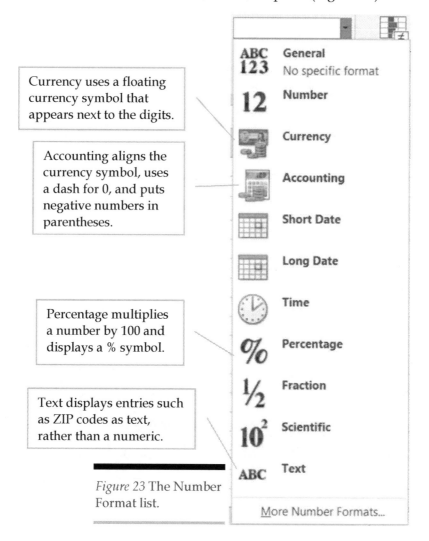

Currency uses a floating currency symbol that appears next to the digits.

Accounting aligns the currency symbol, uses a dash for 0, and puts negative numbers in parentheses.

Percentage multiplies a number by 100 and displays a % symbol.

Text displays entries such as ZIP codes as text, rather than a numeric.

Figure 23 The Number Format list.

Or

Click the Number Format dialog box launcher in the Number group on the Home tab and then set options in the dialog box (Figure 24).

Figure 24 The Format Cells dialog box.

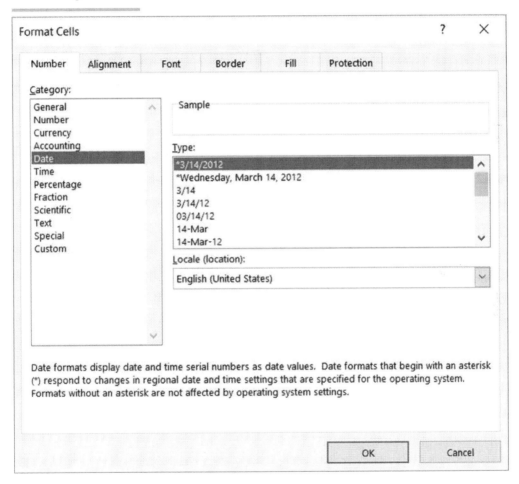

3. *Optional.* Click formatting commands in the Number group on the Home tab to set accounting format, format as a percent, use a comma separator, and control the decimal places. (Figure 25.)

Figure 25 The Number group commands on the Home tab.

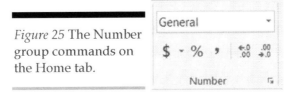

TIP If formatting a value displays ##### in a cell, simply widen the column.

TIP Typing a $ or % with a number automatically formats a cell. However, data entry is often faster when you enter numbers and format cells after (or before). When a number less than 1 is entered into an empty cell formatted as percent, the number is multiplied by 100.

TIP When entering text made up of numbers, such as a ZIP code, format cells as Text from the Number Format list *before* typing data, or select the Special format from the Format Cells dialog box.

TIP To remove formatting from numeric data, click Home ⇨ Clear ⇨ Clear Formats or change the formatting to General. Changing a date or time to General format displays a numeric value representing elapsed days since January 0, 1900.

Conditional Formatting

Conditional formatting adds color, data bars, or icons to cells based on the relative values in a selected range. Figure 26 shows conditional formatting applied to each stock analysis.

Figure 26 Conditional formatting provides a visual interpretation.

	A	B	C	D	E	F	G
1			Portfolio 2016				
2							
3		Ticker	End of Month Close Price				
4	Stock	Symbol	Jan	Apr	Jul	Oct	Dec
5	Amazon	AMZN	$587.00	$659.59	$758.81	$789.82	$749.87
6	Microsoft	MSFT	$55.09	$49.87	$56.68	$59.92	$62.14
7	Google	GOOG	$742.95	$693.01	$768.79	$784.54	$771.82

To apply conditional formatting:

1. Select the range to format. Note that the values in the range will be compared relative to one another, so the range should contain only the values that are logical to compare. For example, in Figure 26 the range C5:G5 was formatted, and then C6:G6, and finally C7:G7.

2. Click Home ⇨ Conditional Formatting. A menu is displayed (Figure 27).

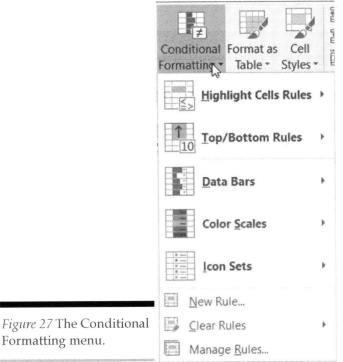

Figure 27 The Conditional Formatting menu.

Or

Click the Quick Analysis button, displayed when a range is selected (Figure 28).

Figure 28 The Quick Analysis menu.

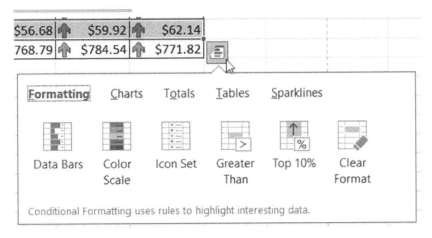

3. Point to a command and then hover over an option for a preview before clicking a format. (The Quick Analysis button has fewer options than Home ⇨ Conditional Formatting.) Refer to Table 12 on pg. 59 for more on relational operators (<, >, =).

4. *Optional*. Click Home ⇨ Conditional Formatting ⇨ Manage Rules, select a rule, and then click Edit Rule to customize how the rule is applied.

TIP Explore the many conditional formatting options and use the Manage Rules command to fine tune the formats so that data is properly conveyed.

TIP More than one conditional format can be applied to a cell range.

Themes and Cell Styles

A *theme* is a named set of colors, fonts, and effects. The default theme is named Office Theme. Selecting a new theme changes the colors, fonts, and effects on a worksheet in a single step. The selected theme on the Page Layout tab also sets the Cell Styles on the Home tab.

To change a theme and apply cell styles:

1. Click Page Layout ⇨ Themes.

2. Hover over an option in the displayed gallery for a preview before clicking a theme.

3. *Optional*. Click Page Layout ⇨ Colors, Page Layout ⇨ Fonts, and Page Layout ⇨ Effects to customize the selected theme.

4. *Optional*. Apply formatting to selected cells by clicking styles on the Home tab. Note that any previously applied styles will change automatically according to the selected theme.

TIP Click Page Layout ⇨ Themes ⇨ Save Current Theme to add a customized theme to the Themes gallery.

The Sheet Tab

A polished, professional workbook will have descriptively named sheets. Color coding the sheet tabs will further improve usability, especially when a workbook contains multiple sheets.

To rename a sheet tab and color code it:

1.   Right-click the sheet tab and click Rename.

2.   Type a new name and then press Enter.

3.   Right-click the sheet tab, click Tab Color, and then select a color.

Format Painter

The Home ⇨ Format Painter command offers a time-saving way to create consistent formats in your spreadsheet. Its ScreenTip serves as a reminder of how to use the command (Figure 29).

Figure 29 The Format Painter command.

To copy and paste formats:

1.   Select the cell with the formats you want to copy.

2.　Click Format Painter. The cell displays a moving border and the mouse pointer displays the Format Painter icon.

3.　Click a different cell or select a range to apply the formats.

TIP If you want to apply the same formats in several locations, double-click Format Painter when copying the formats and then click in each destination location. When you no longer want to paste formats, press the Esc key.

Adding Graphics

Company logos and other illustrations convey information and make a spreadsheet more interesting. Excel has commands for inserting pictures, shapes, SmartArt graphics, text boxes, WordArt, and equations.

To place an illustration on a spreadsheet:

1.　Plan where your image will go. If needed, insert rows and columns to make room. An image will not be stored in a selected cell because images are floating objects on a spreadsheet, but you will probably want an area with empty cells so the image doesn't cover existing data.

2.　If you want to insert a photo or existing graphic, click Insert ⇨ Pictures. A dialog box is displayed.

Or

Click Insert ⇨ Online Pictures. A dialog box is displayed.

3.　If your picture is on one of your storage devices, navigate to the location and then select the image. Images can be in one of many formats, commonly JPEG, TIF, or GIF.

Or

If you're inserting an online picture, type a search word to begin the process of finding a relevant image. (Copyright protects images on the Internet. Click the Creative Commons licenses link in the dialog box for more information.)

The added image displays a rotation handle and size handles on each side and at every corner.

4.　Point to the image until the four-headed move pointer is displayed and then drag the image to the desired location on the spreadsheet. Small images may have a move handle that can be dragged.

5. Drag a size handle on the image edges to size the graphic appropriately. Press and hold the Shift key while dragging a corner handle to maintain the aspect ratio of the image. You can also use the Size commands or click the Size dialog box launcher in the Size group on the Picture Tools Format tab (available when an image is selected).

6. *Optional.* Drag the circular rotation handle on a selected image to rotate it.

7. *Optional.* Use the commands on the Picture Tools Format tab to adjust the image color or change the picture styles, border, and effects.

T I P Click Page Layout ⇨ Background for a dialog box to select an image to repeat for the entire background.

T I P A very large image may greatly increase your spreadsheet file size. If this is an issue, when selecting the image file, click the Insert arrow in the Insert Picture dialog box and select Link to File.

To add shapes, WordArt, SmartArt, and equations to a spreadsheet:

1. Plan where your image will go. If needed, insert rows and columns to make room so that your images don't cover existing data.

2. If you want to insert a shape, click Insert ⇨ Shapes and then click the shape you want. Your pointer changes to a crosshair.

   a) Drag the crosshair pointer on the spreadsheet to create the shape.

   b) Move the shape to the desired location by dragging the center. Change the size of your shape by dragging a handle along the edge. And change the angle by dragging the circular rotation handle.

   c) If the shape you've added is a callout, then a blinking insertion point will be displayed. (Click the center of the callout shape if the insertion point is not displayed.) Type the text for your callout.

   d) Use commands on the Drawing Tools Format tab to further format your shape.

3. If you want to insert WordArt, click Insert ⇨ WordArt and then pick the style you want. A WordArt text box is added.

   a) To move your WordArt text box, drag the edge of the object, not the center where the text is. You can change the angle by dragging the circular rotation handle.

   b) Type your WordArt text. If typing does not replace the text in the box, be sure that the existing text has been selected before typing. You may need to drag a handle to resize the text box to accommodate text. To format text, select text and then use the Font group on the Home tab to apply formats.

   c) Use commands on the Drawing Tools Format tab to format your WordArt text and text box.

4. If you want to insert SmartArt, click Insert ⇨ SmartArt. A dialog box is displayed.

   a) Choose a SmartArt graphic and click OK. A SmartArt graphic is added.

   b) To move your SmartArt, drag the edge of the object, not the center where the objects are. You can change the angle by dragging the circular rotation handle.

   c) A SmartArt graphic displays text boxes where you need text and photo icons where you need images. Click a text box to enter your own text. Click a photo icon to display a dialog box where you can navigate to an image.

   d) A SmartArt graphic is a collection of shapes. Right-click an individual shape and then click Change Shape for shape options, or click Add Shape to extend the SmartArt graphic. Use the handles on selected shapes to rotate or size.

   e) Use commands on the SmartArt Tools Design tab to choose layout and style options. To format individual shapes, use commands on the SmartArt Tools Format tab.

5. If you want to insert an equation, click Insert ⇨ Equation (in the Symbols group). An equation object is added to the spreadsheet and the Equation Tools Design tab is displayed on the Ribbon.

$$A = \pi r^2$$

   a) If you want to use a pre-built equation, click Equation Tools Design ⇨ Equation and then select an existing equation.

   b) If you want to build your own equation, use the symbols and tools on the Equation Tools Design tab.

   c)   To move your equation, drag the edge of the object. Change the angle of the equation by dragging the circular rotation handle.

   d)   Use commands on the Drawing Tools Format tab to choose layout and style options for the equation box.

Text boxes are a useful spreadsheet object for many reasons. They allow you to easily add instructions and messages without having to insert or merge cells. To add text boxes to a spreadsheet:

1.   Plan where your text box will go. If needed, insert rows and columns to make room. A text box will not be inserted into a selected cell because it is a floating object on a spreadsheet, but you will probably want an area with empty cells so the box doesn't cover existing data. (However, there may be times when you want the text box to cover data that requires attention!)

> Katherine, please update.

2.   Click Insert ⇨ Text Box. The mouse pointer changes to an I-beam shape.

3.   Drag the I-beam on the spreadsheet to form the text box. A text box with a blinking insertion point is created.

4.   To move your text box, drag the edge of the object, not the center where the text is. Change the angle of the box by dragging the circular rotation handle.

5.   Type your text. You can use commands on the Home tab to format the text. Use commands on the Drawing Tools Format tab to choose style options for the text box itself.

TIP Use commands in the Arrange group on the Format tab to align objects.

Hiding Rows, Columns, and Sheets

In some situations, you may want to hide spreadsheet data.

To hide a row, column, or sheet:

> Right-click a row number, column letter, or sheet tab and click Hide.
>
> *Or*
>
> Select a cell in the row, column, or sheet to hide and click Home ⇨ Format ⇨ Hide & Unhide and then click the appropriate Hide command.

To unhide a row, column, or sheet:

1. To unhide rows, select the rows above and below the hidden rows and then right-click one of the selected row numbers and click Unhide.

   Or

   Select the rows above and below the hidden row and click Home ⇨ Format ⇨ Hide & Unhide ⇨ Unhide Rows.

2. To unhide columns, select the columns to the right and left of the hidden columns and then right-click one of the selected column letters and click Unhide.

   Or

   Select the columns to the right and left of the hidden column and click Home ⇨ Format ⇨ Hide & Unhide ⇨ Unhide Columns.

3. To unhide a sheet, right-click a visible sheet, click Unhide, and then select the sheet to display from the dialog box.

   Or

   Click Home ⇨ Format ⇨ Hide & Unhide ⇨ Unhide Sheet and then select the sheet to display from the dialog box.

4. To unhide all hidden rows and columns, click the Select All button (to the left of column letter A) and then select the Unhide Rows and then the Unhide Columns commands from Home ⇨ Format ⇨ Hide & Unhide.

TIP You can also hide a row or column by changing the row height or column width to 0.

TIP Hidden data will not be included in a sort or chart.

Sorting

Data analysis often requires organizing data by sorting. You can sort data on numeric, text, date, and time values in ascending (smallest to largest) or descending (largest to smallest) order and on cell color, font color, and cell icon set. Note that if a column contains different types of data or data indented with spaces, your sort results may not be as expected.

To do a quick sort by value:

1. Click in a column that is part of the range of data to sort.

    Or

    Select the range of data to sort.

2. Click Data ⇨ ⬛.

    Or

    Click Data ⇨ ⬛.

    Note that Excel sorts a best guess range of data. If you selected a range that was adjacent to other data, a warning dialog box is displayed. Carefully consider whether you want to sort only the selected range, of if the adjacent data should also be moved when the selected data is sorted.

To do a custom sort:

1. Click in the range of data to sort.

    Or

    Select the range of data to sort.

2. Click Data ⇨ Sort. A dialog box is displayed.

3. Click the arrows to select the Sort by column, the Sort On option (Values, Cell Color, Font Color, Cell Icon), and the Order.

4. *Optional.* Click Add Level to specify a secondary sort. For example, you may want to have rows organized by Last Name and, within that sort, by First Name.

TIP The Sort commands are also on the Home tab.

TIP Sorting data that has leading spaces could produce unexpected results. Click Increase Indent ⬛ when you want to indent data.

TIP Click Data ⇨ Filter to place drop-down lists in the headers of a range of cells. Click an arrow to display commands for sorting and filtering. A *filter* limits displayed rows to those which meet certain criteria. Refer to Chapter 6 for more information.

TIP To make a sort case sensitive, click Data ⇨ Sort ⇨ Options ⇨ Case Sensitive.

TIP To sort by row, click Data ⇨ Sort ⇨ Options ⇨ Sort left to right.

Workbook Views and Page Layout

You can switch between worksheet views by clicking commands on the View tab and icons on the Status bar. With these views, you can control the spreadsheet *pagination*, how the spreadsheet is divided into pages. You can also see the *margins*, the white space that extends from the cells to the page edge.

- Normal is the default spreadsheet view.

- Page Break View shrinks the worksheet in the window and displays heavy lines at the page edges. You can drag these page breaks to change the spreadsheet pagination.

- Page Layout displays your spreadsheet as pages with the margins, headers, and footers showing.

Commands on the Page Layout tab are used to further control a spreadsheet printout. Refer to Table 6.

TIP Click the Page Setup dialog box launcher in the Page Setup group on the Page Layout tab for Page, Margins, Header/Footer, and Sheet options.

Table 6 The Page Layout Tab

Margins	Smaller margins allow more cells to print on a page. Click Margins and then select a preset option or click Custom Margins to set your own margins.
Orientation	Click Orientation and select Portrait to print more rows or Landscape to print more columns per page.
Size	Click Size and then select the printer paper size, if necessary.
Print Area	Select a range and the click Print Area ⇨ Set Print Area to define an area for printing. Click Print Area ⇨ Clear Print Area to restore printing to the entire spreadsheet.
Breaks	Click Breaks ⇨ Insert Page Break to insert a page break above and to the left of the select cell(s). Select Breaks ⇨ Remove Page Break or Breaks ⇨ Reset All Page Breaks to clear breaks.

Print Titles	Displays the Sheet tab in the Page Setup dialog box. Under Print Titles, click in Rows to repeat at top and then click the row number to repeat. Similarly, click Columns to repeat at left and then click the column letter to repeat. You can also drag during selection to repeat multiple rows and columns.
Scale to Fit group	Use commands in this group to scale a spreadsheet for printing. For example, click Width ⇨ 1 page to shrink all the columns at print time so that they fit on one page.
Gridlines	Gridlines refer to the lines that appear around cells. Click Print to include gridlines on a printout. For solid, heavier cell lines, format cells with borders before printing.
Headings	Headings refer to the column letters and cell numbers that appear in a spreadsheet. Click Print to include headings on a printout.

Headers and Footers

Headers and footers allow information such as the file name and date to be added to a spreadsheet printout. The information in a header is repeated on every page, which makes a header ideal for displaying page numbers, titles, dates, and other references. Similarly, a footer appears in the bottom margin area. Each worksheet has three header and footer areas for information.

To add information to the header or footer for a worksheet:

1. Click View ⇨ Page Layout.

   Or

   Click Page Layout on the Status bar.

2. Click in a header or footer area and then click the Header & Footer Tools Design tab, if it is not already displayed.

3. Use the Header & Footer Tools Design tab to add information (refer to Figure 30 and Table 7), and then click a cell to return to your spreadsheet.

TIP You can also click Insert ⇨ Headers & Footers to display the spreadsheet in Page Layout with headers and footers showing.

TIP NEVER manually number the pages in your spreadsheet. Insert a page number into the header or footer for a field code that automatically updates.

Figure 30 The Header & Footer Tools Design tab.

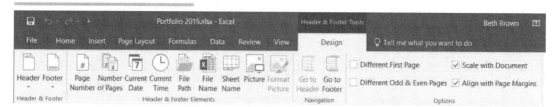

Table 7 The Header & Footer Tools Design Tab

Header	Replaces the current header with a preset one.
Footer	Replaces the current footer with a preset one.
Header & Footer Elements group	Click an option to add a code that automatically inserts the appropriate page number, number of pages, current time, file path, file name, or sheet name.
Picture	Adds a code that inserts a selected graphic from your computer or clip art from the Internet.
Format Picture	Picture formats are limited in the header and footer. Click Format Picture for these options.
Different First Page	Select to allow the headers and footers to vary for the first page.
Different Odd & Even Pages	Select to allow information to vary between odd and even pages.
Scale with Document	Scale header/footer size with spreadsheet when it is scaled to fit.
Align with Page Margins	Select to align headers and footers with margins edges.

Chapter 4
Formulas, Functions, and What-If Analysis

Spreadsheets answer questions through formulas that calculate values based on stored data. If you want to sum a column, then you create a formula. Formulas become even more powerful when they include functions that perform a specific calculation and return a value.

Formulas

A formula must begin with an equal sign so that Excel understands to perform a calculation. Operators in a formula indicate which calculations to perform (Table 8). For example, entering =7 * 3 in a cell automatically displays the result 21. The Formula bar displays the contents of a selected cell, while the cell itself displays the results of a calculation, as in Figure 31.

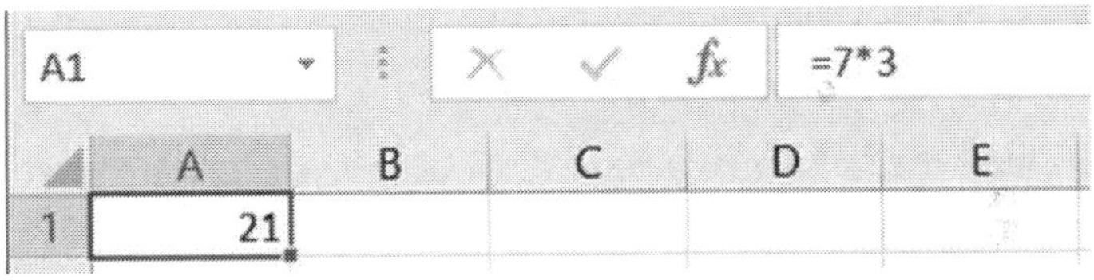

Figure 31 Cell A1 displays the result of a formula.

Table 8 Arithmetic Operators

–	negation
%	percent divides a value by 100
^	exponentiation
*	multiplication
/	division
+	addition
–	subtraction

When evaluating a formula, Excel uses a specific *order of operations*. Negation and percent are performed first. Exponentiation is performed next, and then multiplication and division. Addition and subtraction are performed last. Operators of equal precedence, such as + and –, are performed in order from left to right. For example, =7 + 1 * 2 – 4 evaluates to 5 because the multiplication is performed first and then addition followed by subtraction.

To force a particular order of operations, you use parentheses. Calculations within parentheses are performed first. For example, =(7 + 1) * 2 evaluates to 16.

Errors are indicated by a green triangle in the upper-left corner of a cell. Refer to Table 9 for common formula errors and their causes.

To evaluate a cell with an error:

1.　Select the cell containing the green triangle. The Error Checking button is displayed.

2.　Click the Error Checking button and select an action from the list.

TIP Carefully consider the construction of a formula. Misplacing a parenthesis or misunderstanding the order of operations can result in a hard to detect error that affects the integrity of the entire spreadsheet.

TIP Click File ⇨ Options ⇨ Formulas to review options related to formula calculations and error handling.

TIP If the Formula bar is not displayed, click File ⇨ Options ⇨ Advanced and then click Show formula bar.

Showing Formulas

Show Formulas allows you to view and print the formulas in the cells rather than the results.

To display formulas in their cells:

1.　Click Formulas ⇨ Show Formulas or press Ctrl+`. The ` key is located above the Tab key. Formulas are displayed in cells and the columns widths are adjusted to better view long formulas.

2.　Click Formulas ⇨ Show Formulas or press Ctrl+` again to return to viewing the formula results in cells. Column widths return to their original size.

The Status Bar

The Status bar displays common statistics about a range of data without creating formulas.

To analyze data using the Status bar:

1. Select the range of cells you want to analyze.

2. View the Status bar for immediate results, similar to Figure 32.

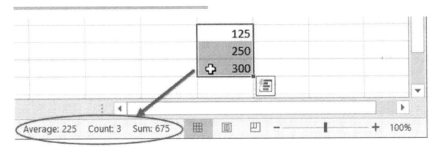

Figure 32 The Status bar displays statistics for selected cells.

3. *Optional.* Right-click the Status bar to view the results and to customize the results displayed, including adding Numerical Count, Minimum, and Maximum.

Cell References

The power of a spreadsheet lies in its ability to refer to other cells in calculations. To create a formula that uses the data in another cell, you use a *cell reference* in the formula. When a value in a referenced cell changes, the formula that includes the reference is automatically recalculated.

To create a formula that uses a cell reference:

1. Select the cell to store the formula.

2.   Type = and then continue with the rest of the formula by typing cell references where a value from another cell should be used. The referenced cell is outlined when typing, as in Figure 33.

		Income	January	
Figure 33 The cell reference was typed.	3	Source	Income	10% Savings
	4	Part-time job	$1,200	=10%*B4

Or

Type = and then continue with the rest of the formula by clicking the cell that should be referenced. This process is called *pointing*, and it avoids typing errors. When you point to a cell, it displays a scrolling outline, as in Figure 34.

		Income	January	
Figure 34 Cell B4 was clicked to enter its reference.	3	Source	Income	10% Savings
	4	Part-time job	⬦$1,200	=10%*B4

3.   Press Enter when the formula is complete. The results are displayed in the cell. If necessary, refer to Table 9 for common formula errors. To edit the formula, click the cell containing the formula and then make edits on the Formula bar. Double-click the cell to make edits within the cell itself.

TIP A *circular reference* error occurs when a formula refers to the cell it is stored in.

TIP References to cells on a different sheet must be preceded by the sheet name, as in Sheet2!B3. You can type or point to enter references on a different sheet.

Table 9 Common Formula Errors

The formula is displayed in the cell	Be sure the formula begins with an equal sign (=) otherwise Excel interprets the data as text.
#####	The formula resulted in a value too large to be displayed in the cell and the column needs to be widened. This error also occurs when the result is a negative date or time.
#DIV/0!	A formula is trying to divide a number by 0 or by a cell that does not contain a value.

#N/A	A formula is trying to reference a value that is not available.
#NAME	Displayed when a formula does not recognize text. Typically, a range name or a function name is spelled incorrectly.
#NULL	Ranges may not be correctly separated in a function.
#NUM	A formula or function contains invalid numeric data.
#REF	The cell or range reference in a formula or function is invalid.
#VALUE	Referenced cells contain an invalid data type for the formula or function.

TIP If a calculation involving dates or times displays an unexpected result, it may be related to the cell format. Click the Number Format dialog box launcher (on the Home tab in the Number group) and click Custom for date and time formats.

Copying and Moving Formulas

Rather than create individual formulas for related data, you can copy the first formula to related cells. When a formula is copied or moved to a new location, cell references automatically change relative to their new location. In Figure 35, when the formula =10%*B4 in cell C4 was copied to cell C5 Excel changed the cell reference to B5. A cell reference that changes when copied is called a *relative cell reference*.

Figure 35 When a formula is copied, cell references change relative to their new location.

| C5 | | | | ✗ | ✓ | *fx* | =10%*B5 |

	A	B	C	D
1			Savings Plan	
3	Income Source	January Income	10% Savings	20% Savings
4	Part-time job	$1,200	$120	
5	Etsy store	$380	✛ $38	

When you want to prevent a cell reference from changing, you will need to use an *absolute reference*. Dollar signs before the column letter and row number indicate the reference is to remain the same when copied. For example, A3 is an absolute reference to cell A3. This reference will not change should the formula containing it be copied to another cell.

Mixed references are a combination of absolute and relative referencing. The reference $A3 means that only the column letter must remain constant. A$3 keeps the row number constant.

To create and then copy a formula from one cell to another:

1. Enter the formula using appropriate cell references. Rather than typing $ for absolute and mixed references, after typing or clicking a cell reference, press F4 to cycle through reference types.

2. Select the cell containing the formula.

3. Click Home ⇨ Copy. A moving border is displayed.

4. Select the cell to receive the copy.

5. Click Home ⇨ Paste. The formula is copied and cell references are changed to reflect the new location.

6. *Optional.* Click Paste Options that appears in the lower-right of the destination cell and select an option. Refer to Table 10.

TIP To move cell contents, use the Cut and Paste commands or drag a cell using the four-headed move pointer (pg. 23).

Table 10 Paste Options

	Paste. The default paste option. Paste all source cell contents.
	Formulas. Paste only formulas without source formatting.
	Formulas and Number Formatting. Paste only formulas and number formats.
	Keep Source Formatting. Paste contents and source formats.
	No Borders. Paste all contents except border formats.
	Keep Source Column Widths. Paste contents and match source column width.

	Transpose. Transposes a range of data from rows to columns or vice versa.
	Values. Paste only the value displayed in the source cell, not the formula.
	Values & Number Formatting. Paste only the value and applied numeric formats, not the formula.
	Values & Source Formatting. Paste only the value and source cell formats, not the formula.
	Formatting. Paste only source cell formats, not the contents.
	Paste Link. Paste a reference to the source cell.
	Picture. Paste an image of the source cell.
	Linked Picture. Paste an image of the source cell that updates if changes are made.

Filling a Range

A better way to copy formulas to adjacent cells is to drag the fill handle.

To copy a formula to a range of cells:

1. Enter the formula using appropriate cell references.

2. Select the cell containing the formula.

3. Drag the fill handle down and/or across to copy the formula, as in Figure 36.

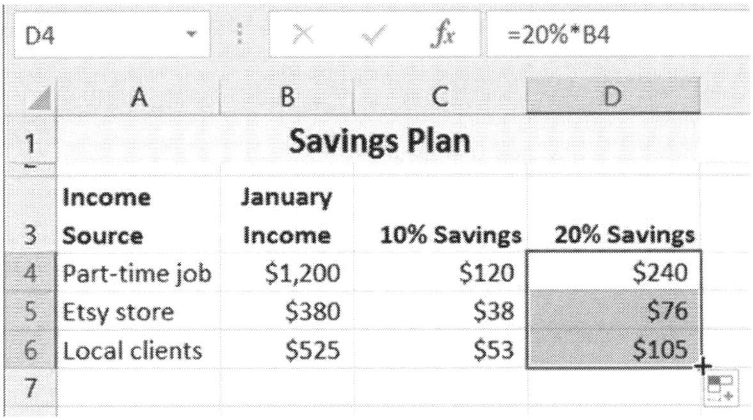

		A	B	C	D
	1			Savings Plan	
	3	Income Source	January Income	10% Savings	20% Savings
	4	Part-time job	$1,200	$120	$240
	5	Etsy store	$380	$38	$76
	6	Local clients	$525	$53	$105
	7				

D4   fx   =20%*B4

Figure 36 Drag the fill handle to copy a formula.

Or

Select the range of cells to fill and then click the appropriate command from Home ⇨ Fill. This technique is especially useful when you have a large range of cells to fill.

4. *Optional.* Click Auto Fill Options and select an option, similar to Figure 37.

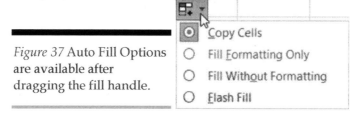

Figure 37 Auto Fill Options are available after dragging the fill handle.

Functions

Functions perform a specific calculation and then return a single value. Most functions require *arguments*, values that are used to perform the calculation. A single formula can contain numerous functions to perform sophisticated calculations. One of the most commonly used functions is SUM, and it can be used in formulas like:

=SUM(A3:A6)

=SUM(A10, B12, D2)

=B12 - SUM(C4:C7)

=SUM(Sheet1:Sheet4!C7)

SUM adds up the values in the supplied arguments to return a single value. Note that arguments are enclosed in parentheses. Arguments can be in the form of a range of cells or a series of cells separated by commas. In the last example, cell C7 from Sheet1 through Sheet4 will be summed. This is called a 3D SUM.

When you type a function, Excel displays an Intellisense function guide to remind you of the needed arguments (Figure 38). Optional arguments are in brackets:

Figure 38 The Intellisense function guide.

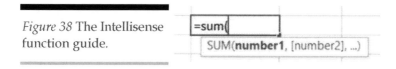

To create a formula with a function:

1. Select the cell to store the formula.

2. Type = and then continue with the rest of the formula by typing references and operators and by inserting functions and their arguments where needed (Table 11 lists some Excel functions). Use one of the following three methods to insert a function:

> METHOD 1: Type the function name and the open parenthesis and then enter the arguments by clicking cell references, selecting cell ranges (Figure 39), or by typing data. Multiple arguments must be separated by commas.

	A	B
1		**Savings**
	Income	**January**
3	**Source**	**Income** 10
4	Part-time job	$1,200
5	Etsy store	$380
6	Local clients	✛ $525
7	Total	=sum(B4:B6)

Figure 39 The mouse was used to select the cell range for the argument.

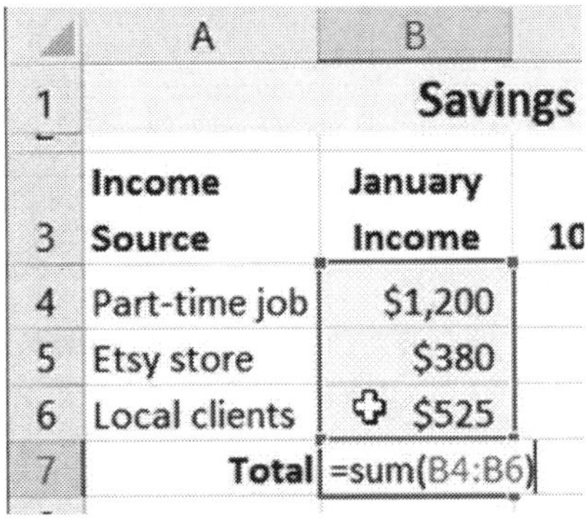

> METHOD 2: Click an arrow for one of the commands in the Function Library group on the Formulas tab (Figure 42) and then click a function name, which displays the Function Arguments dialog box (Figure 40).

Figure 40 Click **Formulas** ⇨ **Math & Trig** ⇨ **Sum** to display this dialog box.

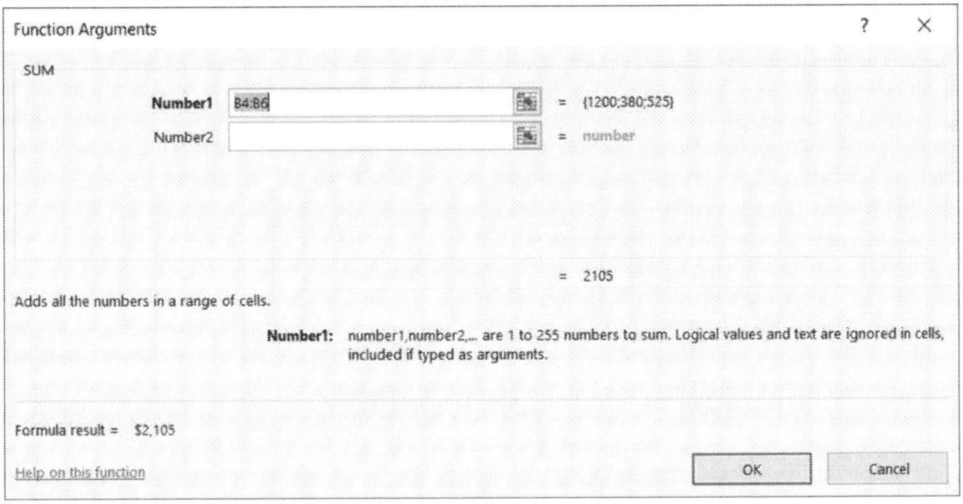

Function Arguments   ?   ✕

SUM

    Number1 B4:B6   = {1200;380;525}

    Number2   = number

= 2105

Adds all the numbers in a range of cells.

    Number1: number1,number2,... are 1 to 255 numbers to sum. Logical values and text are ignored in cells, included if typed as arguments.

Formula result = $2,105

Help on this function   OK   Cancel

METHOD 3: Click Formulas ⇨ Insert Function. A dialog box is displayed where you type a description of what you want the function to do and then click Go (Figure 41).

Figure 41 The Insert Function dialog box.

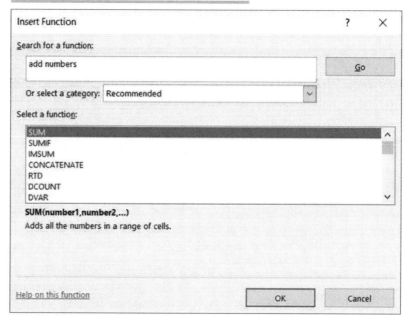

Next, click a formula in the list and OK to display the Function Arguments dialog box (Figure 40).

3. If using the Function Arguments dialog box, click in the first argument box and then type or select the cell or range for the argument. Repeat this process for each argument. Select OK to insert the function.

TIP To select nonadjacent cells with the mouse, press and hold the Ctrl key while clicking cells or ranges.

Figure 42 The Function Library group.

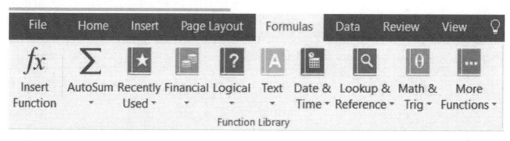

Table 11 Excel Functions (limited list)

Type "Excel functions" in the Tell Me box, click the Get Help on command, and then click Excel functions (by category) for a complete list.

SUM	Returns the sum of its numeric arguments, ignoring text values. (Math & Trig)
IF	Performs an action based on a logical test. (Logical)
LOOKUP	Uses it first argument, the lookup value, to find a match in one row or column and then returns the corresponding value one row or column over. (Lookup & Reference)
VLOOKUP	Use its first argument, the lookup value, to find a match in the first column of a range and then move across the row to return the next value over. (Lookup & Reference)
MATCH	Returns the relative position of a specified value within a range. (Lookup & Reference)
CHOOSE	Uses the value of its first argument to determine which of its remaining arguments to return. Arguments can be a value, cell reference, or range reference. (Lookup & Reference)
DATE	Combines year, month, and day arguments to return a complete date. (Date & Time)
DAYS	Returns the number of days between two dates. (Date & Time)
FIND, FINDB	Locates a text string within a second text string and returns the starting position. FINDB supports Japanese, Chinese, and Korean languages. (Text)
INDEX	Returns the value at the intersection of a row and column argument. (Lookup & Reference)
CONVERT	Converts a numeric argument from one measurement system to another. (More Functions ⇨ Engineering)
FV	Returns the future value of an investment. (Financial)
PMT	Returns the periodic payments for an annuity. (Financial)

ISBLANK	Returns TRUE if a cell is blank. (More Functions ⇨ Information)
DEGREES	Converts radians to degrees. (Math)
RAND	Returns a random number between 0 and 1. (Math)
ROUND	Rounds a number to a specified number of decimal places. (Math)
TRIM	Removes spaces from around text. This function is important when sorting text that may have leading spaces. (Text)
ISTEXT	Returns TRUE if a value is text. (More Functions ⇨ Information)

The AutoSum Command

The SUM, AVERAGE, COUNT, MAX, and MIN functions are so commonly used that Excel provides the AutoSum command on both the Home tab and the Formulas tab. With one click, you can insert a formula with one of these functions.

There are two ways to use AutoSum to insert a formula with a function:

METHOD 1: Select a range for the function arguments

1. Select the cells to sum. If the selected cells are in a column, be sure there is an empty cell below the selected range. If the selected cells are in a row, be sure there is an empty cell to the right of the selected range.

2. Click Home ⇨ AutoSum. The sum of the cells is displayed in the cell adjacent to the selected range.

   Or

   Click the Home ⇨ AutoSum arrow and then click a function. The result of the formula with the selected function is displayed in the cell adjacent to the range.

   Or

    Click the Quick Analysis button in the lower-right corner of the selected range, click the Totals tab, and select an option.

METHOD 2: Select a cell to insert the formula

1. Select the cell to store the AutoSum formula.

2. Click Home ⇨ AutoSum. Excel highlights a best guess range.

    Or

    Click the Home ⇨ AutoSum arrow and then click a function. Excel highlights a best guess range.

3. If the range is incorrect, use the mouse to select the correct range, or use the arrow keys to select the first cell in the range and then press and hold Shift while pressing the arrow keys to extend the selection.

4. Press Enter.

TIP Clicking Home ⇨ AutoSum ⇨ More Functions will place a formula in the first cell of a selected range (probably not what you want with AutoSum).

Defining Names

Defined names provide a more meaningful description of the data stored in a cell or cell range. Using defined names in functions make formulas easier to understand. For example, compare =SUM(B3:B10) to =SUM(MaySales).

To create a defined name for a cell or cell range:

1. Select the cell or cell range to name.

2. Click in the Name box and type to replace the current name, as shown in Figure 43.

Figure 43 The Name box with a defined name.

Or

Click Formulas ⇨ Define Name. A dialog box is displayed where you type the defined name.

TIP A defined name must begin with a letter, underscore (_), or backslash (\). It can include only letters, numbers, periods, and the underscore. Spaces are not permitted, and a defined name must be no more than 255 characters.

To use and manage defined names:

- If you want to use a defined name in a function, simply type the defined name as the argument. If you cannot remember the name, click Formulas ⇨ Use in Formula and then click a name to insert it.
- If you defined names after creating formulas that use the same range, select cells containing formulas and click Formulas ⇨ Define Name ⇨ Apply Name to convert any matching ranges to defined names.
- To define a name for a labeled column or row of data, select the range, including the label, and click Formulas ⇨ Create From Selection.
- Click Formulas ⇨ Name Manager to create, edit, or delete defined names.

The IF Function

The IF function is one of the logical functions provided in Excel, and one of the most popular functions used. IF uses a logical test to determine which action to perform. When the test is TRUE, the first action is performed. A FALSE test means the second action will be performed. Formulas with an IF can appear like:

=IF(B4>=100, "Commission", "No commission")

=IF(SUM(C4:C8)<250, D3, E3)

=IF(AND(SUM(E64:E90)>50, SUM(G64:G90)>75), "Target Reached", " ")

Note that functions can *nest* other functions as arguments, as in the second and third examples above. The last example includes an AND function, another logical function, which is TRUE when all its arguments are true. Table 13 lists logical functions.

TIP An IF function returns FALSE when a logical test is false and a false value hasn't been provided.

TIP You can nest functions up to 64 levels. However, deep nesting may be better handled with a different type of function. For example, the logic of multiple IFs may be improved with a VLOOKUP, CHOOSE, or SWITCH function.

To create a formula with an IF function:

1.   Select the cell to store the formula.

2.   Type =IF(and then enter the logical test. The logical test uses a comparison operator (Table 12), or a logical function (Table 13) when two or more comparisons are to be used to determine the outcome of the logical test.

3.   Type a comma after the logical test argument and then enter the TRUE action followed by a comma and then the FALSE action. The TRUE and FALSE actions can also include nested functions.

4.   Type the closing parenthesis and press Enter. Excel will try to alert you to mismatched parentheses and other common errors with complex functions.

Table 12 Comparison Operators

=	equal
<	less than
>	greater than
<=	less than or equal to
>=	greater than or equal to
<>	not equal to

Table 13 Logical Functions

IF	Performs an action based on a logical test. (Logical)
AND	Returns TRUE when all arguments are true. (Logical)
OR	Returns TRUE when at least one argument is true. (Logical)
NOT	Reverses the logic of its argument. (Logical)

Formula Auditing

Formulas can become complex. Tools for tracing the cells related to a formula are available in the Formula Auditing group on the Formulas tab (Figure 44, Table 14).

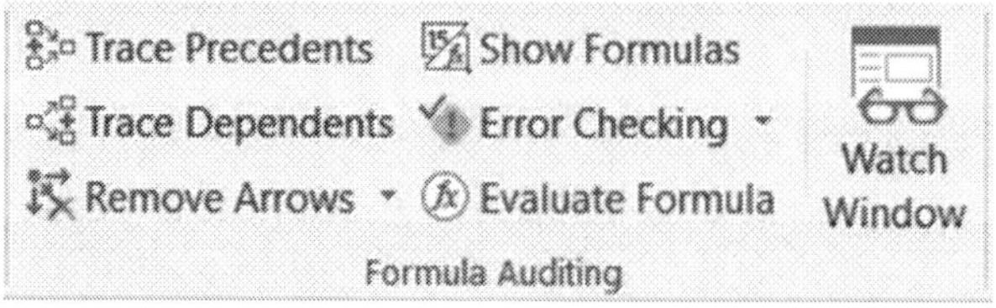

Figure 44 The Formula Auditing group.

Table 14 Formula Auditing

Trace Precedents	Displays arrows from cells used in a formula to the selected cell.
Trace Dependents	Displays arrows to cells affected by the formula in the selected cell.
Remove Arrows	Hides displayed arrows.
Show Formulas	Displays formulas in cells rather than results. See also page 46.
Error Checking	Checks a spreadsheet for errors. Click Error Checking ⇨ Trace Error to display arrows from precedents to dependents. Click Error Checking ⇨ Circular References for a list of circular references.
Evaluate Formula	Displays a dialog box for debugging and stepping through a formula.
Watch Window	Used to create a list of cell values that update as spreadsheet values change.

Data Validation

Data validation helps ensure accuracy and improves the integrity of a spreadsheet. When cells have validation rules, users can enter only data that meet these rules.

To create validation rules for a cell:

1. Select a cell or range of cells for the rules.

2.   Click Data ⇨ Data Validation. A dialog box is displayed.

3.   Click the Allow list and select the basic entry type.

4.   If you selected List, type the list entries separated by commas into the Source box (You can also select a range of cells on the spreadsheet containing valid entries or compare to a named range with a formula, for example, =Products). Skip ahead to Step 8.

5.   If you selected Custom, type the formula that will determine validity into the Formula box, for example, =ISTEXT(C3). Skip ahead to Step 8.

6.   Click Data and select the range operator for the allowable data.

7.   Type values for the data range. (Values can be cell contents, such as =C11, or formulas with functions, such as =TODAY().)

8.   Click the Input Message tab and type a title and input message describing the type of entry expected.

9.   Click the Error Alert tab to create an error message that is displayed when there is an attempt to enter invalid data.

TIP You can apply data validation to cells that already contain data. In this case, a green indicator appears in cells that don't meet validation rules. Click Data Validation ⇨ Circle Invalid Data to display red circles around invalid data.

TIP Click Data ⇨ Data Validation again to edit validation rules. Select the Apply these changes to all other cells with the same settings option to make changes to all cells with the same validation rules.

What-If? Analysis

After building your spreadsheet model, you can change values to ask What if? What if my costs change? How will this affect my bottom line? Or, how must related values change in order to double my profit? Excel has Scenario Manager, Goal Seek, and Data Table commands on the Data tab for performing *What-If? analysis*.

A *scenario* allows you to see various outcomes based on defined data sets. To create and use scenarios:

1.   Decide which cells you want to change in order to ask What if?

Consider the spreadsheet in Figure 45. Next Level Tacos sells out of their signature fish tacos every day. The owner wants to find a new fish supplier that can provide more fish daily so that Next Level can increase their taco sales. The owner asks: What if I use Day Boat A that will provide enough fish for 90 tacos at a cost of $2.00 per taco? Or what if I use Day Boat B that provides enough fish for 100 tacos at a cost of $2.25 per taco? The cells that will change to answer these questions are B6 and D6.

Figure 45 The spreadsheet shows current taco sales.

	A	B	C	D	E
1	Next Level Tacos Food Truck				
2					
3	Menu Item	Cost	Price	Units Sold/Day	Profit
4	Chicken Taco	$0.80	$3.00	35	$77.00
5	Beef Taco	$0.95	$4.00	50	$152.50
6	Fish Taco	$1.80	$6.00	80	$336.00
7				Total	$565.50

2. To make the scenario summary easier to interpret later, define names for the cells that will change and for the cells that will display new output.

   For example, for the Next Level spreadsheet in Figure 45, cell B6 was named FishCost, cell D6 FishUnits, cell E6 FishProfits, and cell E7 TotalProfit.

3. Click Data ⇨ What-If Analysis ⇨ Scenario Manager. A dialog box is displayed.

4. Click Add. Type the Scenario name, click in the Changing cells box, and type the changing cell names. (You may also click the spreadsheet to add cells to the box, or click the cell selection dialog at the end of the box.) Figure 46 shows the Add Scenario dialog box for a Next Level Tacos scenario.

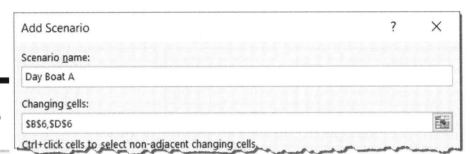

Figure 46 The
Add Scenario
dialog box.

5. Click OK. The Scenario Values dialog box is displayed. Type the values for the scenario and then click OK.

   For example, for the Day Boat A scenario, the FishCost (B6) is 2.00 and FishUnits is 90.

6. Repeat steps 4 and 5 to add additional scenarios. You can have up to 32 changing cells in each scenario.

7. To display the effects of a scenario, click the scenario name and then click Show.

8. To compare all the scenarios, click Summary, select the cells with changing outputs, and then click OK. The summary is added to a new sheet. Figure 47 compares the two Next Level scenarios.

Figure 47 Scenario Summary
for Next Level Tacos.

		Current Values:	Day Boat A	Day Boat B
Scenario Summary				
Changing Cells:				
FishCost		$1.80	$2.00	$2.25
FishUnits		80	90	100
Result Cells:				
FishProfits		$336.00	$360.00	$375.00
TotalProfit		$565.50	$589.50	$604.50

Notes: Current Values column represents values of changing cells at time Scenario Summary Report was created. Changing cells for each scenario are highlighted in gray.

Goal Seek allows you to determine the input for reaching a goal. To goal seek:

1. Decide which cell should contain the goal value.

    For example, using the spreadsheet in Figure 45 above, the Next Level Tacos owner wants to know how much to increase the chicken taco price in order to bring the profit up to $100. The cell to contain the goal value is E4.

2. Click Data ⇨ What-If Analysis ⇨ Goal Seek. A dialog box is displayed.

3. Enter the Set cell (from Step 1), type the To value, select or type the By changing cell.

    Figure 48 shows the goal seek for Next Level Tacos.

Figure 48 How much should Next Level charge for chicken tacos for a $100 profit?

▲	A	B	C	D	E
1	**Next Level Tacos Food Truck**				
2					
3	**Menu Item**	**Cost**	**Price**	**Units Sold/Day**	**Profit**
4	Chicken Taco	$0.80	$3.00	35	$77.00
5	Beef Taco	$0.95	$4.00	50	$152.50
6	Fish Taco	$1.	*Goal Seek*	? ✕	
7					
8			Set cell:	E4	
9			To value:	100	
10			By changing cell:	C4	
11					
12			OK	Cancel	
13					

4. Click OK. The changing cell displays the value to reach the goal.

    Figure 49 shows the goal seek results for Next Level Tacos.

Figure 49 Profits will increase to $100 when chicken tacos are priced at $3.66.

Menu Item	Cost	Price	Units Sold/Day	Profit
Chicken Taco	$0.80	$3.66	35	$100.00
Beef Taco	$0.95	$4.00	50	$152.50

A *data table* allows you to test one or two different sets of values in a formula. To use a data table to test one set of values:

1. To test a table of values, you must leave room for the data values and their corresponding results. To do this, enter the formula to test in a cell that is at least one column over and one row above the data values it references.

    For example, consider the spreadsheet in Figure 50. Auto loan payments can be calculated using the PMT function, which requires arguments for interest rate, term, and loan amount.

D2			✕	✓	*fx*	=PMT(B3,B4,-B5)

Figure 50 Cells C3:D5 are for the data table. The formula is at the top of the results column.

◢	A	B	C	D
1	**Auto Loan**			**Payment**
2				$836.68
3	Interest Rate	3.75%		
4	Term (months)	48		
5	Loan Amount	$18,500		

2. Type the table in in the column to the left of the test cell (in this case, the PMT formula).

    Figure 51 is set up to test interest rates.

Figure 51 The test data is entered in the first column of the table.

◢	A	B	C	D
1	**Auto Loan**			**Payment**
2				$836.68
3	Interest Rate	3.75%	2.75%	
4	Term (months)	48	3.00%	
5	Loan Amount	$18,500	3.25%	

3. Select the entire table and then click What-If Analysis ⇨ Data Table. A dialog box is displayed (refer to Figure 52).

4. Click the Column input cell (since your data is placed into a column) and then type or select the cell reference to substitute test values for.

    Figure 52 designates the interest rate reference as the one to test with the data values. If the table contained 12, 24, 36, then cell B4 (the term) would be the one to test.

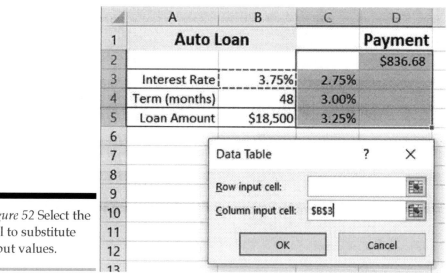

Figure 52 Select the cell to substitute input values.

5. Click OK in the Data Table dialog box to display the results, similar to Figure 53.

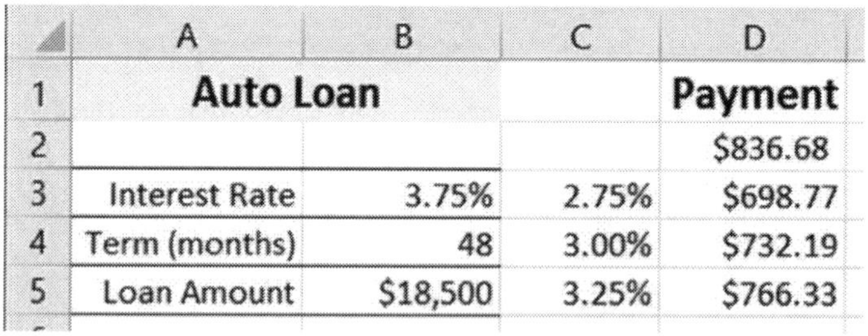

	A	B	C	D
1	**Auto Loan**			**Payment**
2				$836.68
3	Interest Rate	3.75%	2.75%	$698.77
4	Term (months)	48	3.00%	$732.19
5	Loan Amount	$18,500	3.25%	$766.33

Figure 53 The second column of the data table shows results.

TIP Type "data table" in the Tell Me box for help on testing two sets of data.

Chapter 5
Charts

Sometimes the easiest way to understand data relationships is through charts.

Sparklines

Sparklines are tiny charts inside single cells. They are typically placed next to a data series and are useful for showing trends (Figure 54).

Product	Q1	Q2	Q3	Q4	
Blue Gadget	$220	$180	$260	$300	▄ ▃ ▆ █

Figure 54 A Column sparkline.

To create sparklines:

1. Select the cell range to be charted. Be sure there is an empty cell to the right of the selected cells.

2. Click the Quick Analysis button in the lower-right corner of the selected range, click the Sparklines tab, and select a chart type.

3. *Optional.* With a sparkline selected, use commands on the Sparkline Tools Design tab to change the color, type, or customize how data is displayed (Table 15).

TIP You can add a sparkline anywhere. Select the cell for the sparkline and then click a command in the Sparklines group on the Insert tab.

Table 15 Sparkline Tools Design Tab

Note: Multiple sparklines in a column will automatically be grouped so that style changes are consistent.

Edit Data	Select commands to edit the data range and placement of a single sparkline or a group of sparklines. Use the Hidden & Empty Cells command to change how that type of data is handled.
Type group	Click a command to change the sparkline type.

Show group	
	Click an option to emphasize selected data points or to add markers to a line sparkline.
Style group	Select a different sparkline color or marker color.
Axis	Click for commands to show a horizontal axis, set the minimum value, and set the maximum value.
	A sparkline with axis showing.
Group, Ungroup	Group or ungroup sparklines. Grouped sparklines will share applied formatting.
Clear	Click to remove a selected sparkline or sparkline group.

The Recommended Charts Command

A chart is based on one or more *data series* (y values) and corresponding *category labels* (x values). The appropriate chart type usually depends on the way data is arranged and the number of data series. The Insert ⇨ Recommended Charts command suggests chart types based on the selected data.

When deciding on a chart type, ask yourself what the purpose of the chart is. Should it compare data (bar chart)? Show a trend over time (line graph)? Or explain data as parts of a whole (pie chart)? Other chart types are explained in Table 17.

To create a chart using the Recommended Charts command:

1. Click in the range of data to be charted.

    Or

    Highlight the range of data to be charted. For non-contiguous data, press and hold Ctrl while selecting each data series.

2. Click Insert ⇨ Recommended Charts. A dialog box is displayed, similar to Figure 55.

Figure 55 The Insert Chart dialog box.

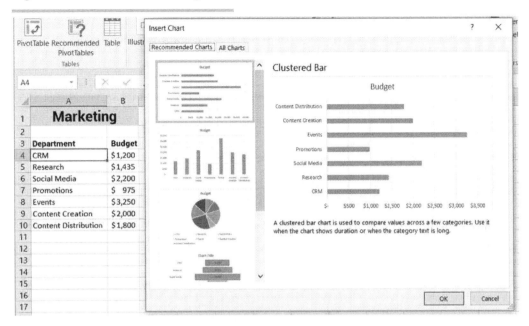

3. Click a chart type in the left pane of the dialog box for a preview. Or click the **All Charts** tab for more chart types.

4. With the desired chart type selected, click **OK**. The chart is added as an object to the worksheet, similar to Figure 56.

Figure 56 A new chart.

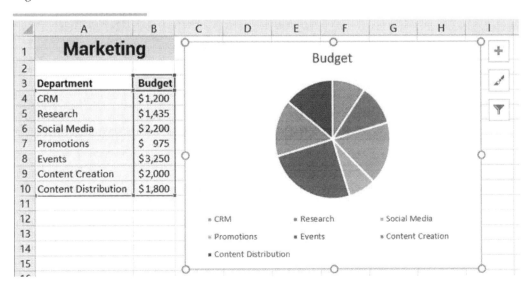

5. Click the chart, if necessary, to make it active so that the chart tools buttons are available:

    ⊞ Click Chart Elements and then click a checkbox to add or remove titles, legends, labels, and so on. Point to an option and click the arrow for placement commands and the More Options command, which displays a Format pane.

    ✎ Click Chart Styles to change the style and color of the chart.

    ▼ Click Chart Filters to change the data used for the chart.

6. *Optional*. Drag a corner handle on chart to size the object. To move the chart, drag the edge with the four-headed move pointer. Select a chart and then press Delete to remove it.

7. *Optional*. A chart is a collection of graphic objects. For example, you can click an individual pie slice and then drag it away from the other slices. To format text within an object, first double-click to place the insertion point.

8. *Optional*. Use commands on the Chart Tools Design tab to choose layout and style options (Table 16).

9. *Optional*. Use commands on the Chart Tools Format tab to format individual objects (Table 16).

10. *Optional*. Refer to "Editing a Chart" on page 74 for advanced editing techniques.

TIP When you highlight a range of data for a chart you can click the Quick Analysis button for recommended chart types.

Table 16 Chart Tools Tabs

Chart Tools Design Tab

Add Chart Element	Commands to add, remove, and change the placement of titles, labels, legends, and more. Click More Options in any submenu to display a Format pane.
Quick Layout	Displays a menu of suggested layouts.
Change Colors	Displays available color palettes.

Chart Styles group	Click the More button in the Chart Styles group for a gallery of styles. Point to a style to preview the effect. Click a style to apply it.
Switch Row/Column	Reverses the data over the axis.
Select Data	Displays a dialog box for changing the data range for the chart.
Change Chart Type	Displays a dialog box for changing the chart type.
Move Chart	Displays a dialog box that prompts you to choose a sheet location for the chart.

Chart Tools Format Tab

Chart Elements list	Chart Area / Chart Area / Chart Title / Legend / Plot Area / Series "Budget"	Click the list arrow to display the elements of your chart. The series elements will vary. Click an element to make it active for formatting.
Format Selection		Display a Format pane with options for the selected element. See "Editing a Chart" (pg. 74).
Reset to Match Style		Clears custom formatting for a selected element.
Insert Shapes group		Click a shape and then drag in the chart area to create a custom object.
Shape Styles group		Select an element and then use the Shape Styles group to customize formatting.
WordArt Styles group		Select an element and then use the WordArt Styles group to customize the look of text.
Arrange group		Click Selection Pane to display a pane where objects on the sheet can be selected. Use the arrangement commands to position the object.
Size group		Change the dimensions of the chart. Click the Size task pane launcher (in the lower-right corner of the group) for more options.

Choosing a Chart Type

There are numerous chart commands on the Insert tab, as summarized in Table 17. Additionally, the ScreenTips for chart commands are especially helpful for deciding the appropriate chart type (Figure 57). You need only point to a chart command to display its ScreenTip. (If your ScreenTips don't pop up, change your preferences in File ⇨ Options ⇨ General.) Click the arrow next to a chart command and then point to a sub chart type for more information there.

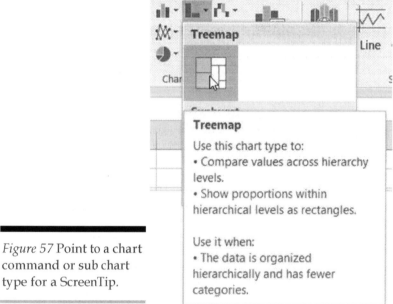

Figure 57 Point to a chart command or sub chart type for a ScreenTip.

To create a chart using an Insert tab chart command:

1. Select a cell in the range of data to be charted.

   Or

   Highlight the range of data to be charted. For non-contiguous data, press and hold Ctrl while selecting each data series.

2. Click the Insert tab.

3. Click a chart command (Table 17). A chart of the selected type is inserted.

   Or

   Click the arrow next to a chart command and then click a sub chart type (Table 17). A chart of the selected type is inserted.

4. Refer to steps 5 through 10 in "The Recommended Charts Command" section on pg. 70.

Table 17 Insert Tab Chart Types

	Column or Bar Chart. A *column chart* has vertical bars, while a *bar chart* has horizontal bars. These charts are useful for comparing values and can include multiple data series. Variations include 3-D Column and 3-D Bar (see example on pg. 78).
	Line or Area Chart. A *line chart* is often used to show a data trend. An *area chart* is filled below the line for additional impact. Variations include 3-D Line and 3-D Area.
	Pie or Doughnut Chart. The *pie chart* shows one data series with each slice as a percentage of the total. The *doughnut chart* can compare one or more data series, showing a series as portions of a circle. There are 3-D variations for both.
	Hierarchy Chart. The *treemap* shows proportions within a rectangle and works best with fewer categories (see example on pg. 77). The *sunburst* shows proportions within rings and can compare more categories. Chart data should be organized into levels.
	Statistic Chart. The *histogram* shows data frequency grouped by bin numbers (intervals). To define bin numbers, right-click the horizontal axis, click Format Axis, and then click Axis Options in the task pane. The *Pareto* is a sorted histogram. The *box and whisker chart* shows distribution of data into quartiles. To customize the chart, right-click a box and click Format Data Series.

Scatter (X, Y) or Bubble Chart. The *scatter chart* is used to plot data points. Chart data must be organized into x values and y values. Variations on the scatter chart connect data points with straight lines or smooth curves. The *bubble chart* adds a third dimension to the scatter chart by sizing data points based on a third column of data, much like a pie chart sizes slices. Bubble charts work best with four or more data points.

Waterfall or Stock Chart. The *waterfall chart* analyzes data through a cumulative effect and is especially useful for visualizing financial statements (see example on pg. 78). To effectively illustrate data, you must designate balance values. To do this, right-click a data point and click Set as Total (to reverse this action, right-click and select Clear Total). The *funnel chart* is best for data that is progressively decreasing. The *stock chart* requires data organized into high, low, and close values and illustrates fluctuations in data. Variations for this chart can include open and volume prices.

Combo Chart. The combo chart uses a different chart for each series. To choose the chart type for a series, click the Combo Chart arrow and select Create Custom Combo Chart.

Surface or Radar Chart. A *surface chart* plots data as a 3-D surface and is helpful for identifying trends and is best when categories and series are both numeric. A *radar chart* compares many independent values that are based on the same starting point (e.g., 0 as a center point).

Editing a Chart

There are many ways to customize a chart after you've decided on the chart type. Along with the Chart Tools tabs, Excel provides formatting panes with even more options.

To edit chart formats:

1. Right-click a chart element and then click a Format command at the bottom of the menu. A corresponding task pane is opened.

   Or

   Double-click a chart element. A corresponding task pane is opened.

   Or

   With the chart active (handles are displayed), select an element from the Chart Elements list on the Chart Tools Format tab and then click Format Selection. A corresponding task pane is opened.

2. Click an icon at the top of the task pane to display related option groups. Figure 58 shows Fill & Line, Effects, Size & Properties, and Axis Options icons.

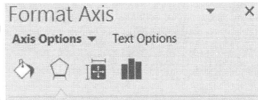

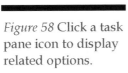
Figure 58 Click a task pane icon to display related options.

3. Below a selected icon, click a white triangle to expand available option groups. Tick Marks has been expanded in Figure 59.

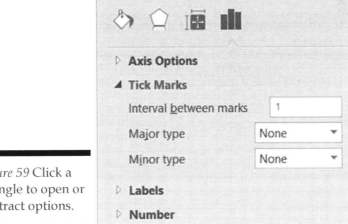

Figure 59 Click a triangle to open or contract options.

4. Change settings as desired.

5. *Optional*. Click Text Options at the top of the task pane, when available, to change text styles.

6. *Optional.* If you want to format a different element on the same chart, click ▼ at the top of the task pane, click an element, and then repeat steps 2 through 5. Refer to Figure 60.

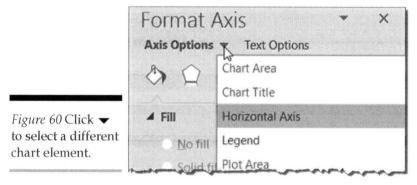

Figure 60 Click ▼ to select a different chart element.

7. Click the X box to close the task pane.

TIP You can also apply specific formats to a single data point. Click a data series on a chart once to select all the data points in the series. Click again to select just a single data point. With the single data point selected, double-click or right-click and select **Format Data Point** to open the corresponding task pane.

TIP An element must first exist in order to format it. To add chart elements, select a chart and then add an element using the **Chart Elements** button.

To edit a chart data series or chart type:

1. Click the chart area to select the chart. The data series and categories in the spreadsheet are also selected.

2. If you want to add a series, drag a corner handle to include adjacent data, as in Figure 61.

Figure 61 Drag the corner handle to the right to add a series to a chart.

	A	B	C
1	Sightings		
2		January	February
3	tree snail	5	9
4	alligator	17	8
5			

Or

Click **Chart Tools Design** ⇨ **Select Data**. A dialog box is displayed.

a. Click in the **Chart data range** box, if the insertion isn't already there.

b. Select the entire series on the spreadsheet, including the new series. If you're adding a nonadjacent series, press and hold the Ctrl key while you select the nonadjacent series.

c. Select OK.

3. If you want to add legends, edit horizontal axis labels, or define how hidden and empty cells should be handled, click Chart Tools Design ⇨ Select Data for a dialog box with related options.

4. If you want to change the chart type, right-click the chart and then click Change Chart Type.

    Or

    Select the chart and click Chart Tools Design ⇨ Change Chart Type.

TIP To print just the chart on a sheet, select the chart before clicking File ⇨ Print. Note the Settings option will be Print Selected Chart. To print a page-sized chart, move a selected chart to its own sheet with Chart Tools Design ⇨ Move Chart before printing.

TIP If you have historical, time-based data, you can create a chart that predicts the future trend by selecting the data range and clicking Data ⇨ Forecast Sheet.

Figure 62 A treemap chart.
Figure 63 A waterfall chart.
Figure 64 A 3-D bar chart.

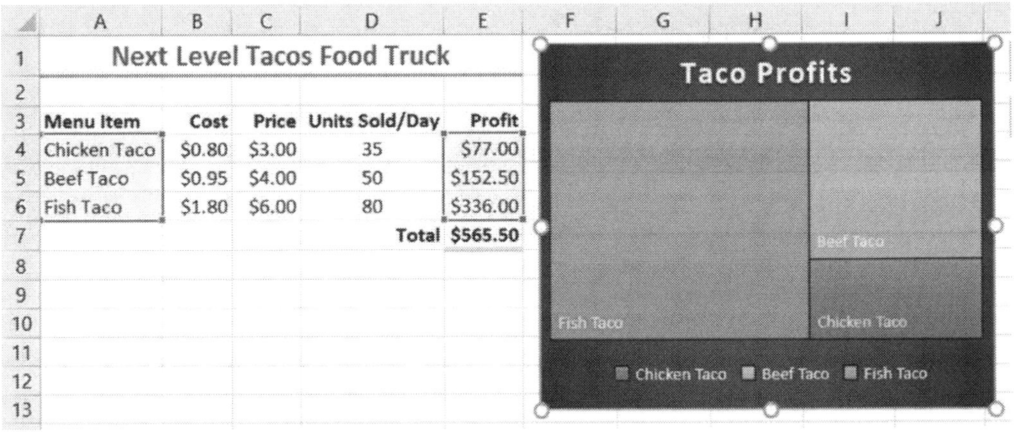

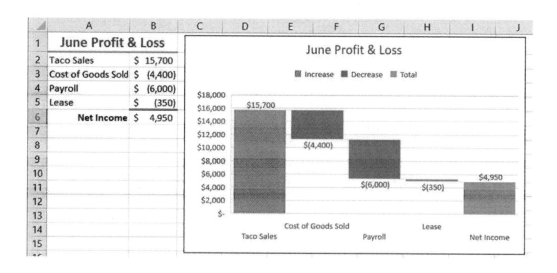

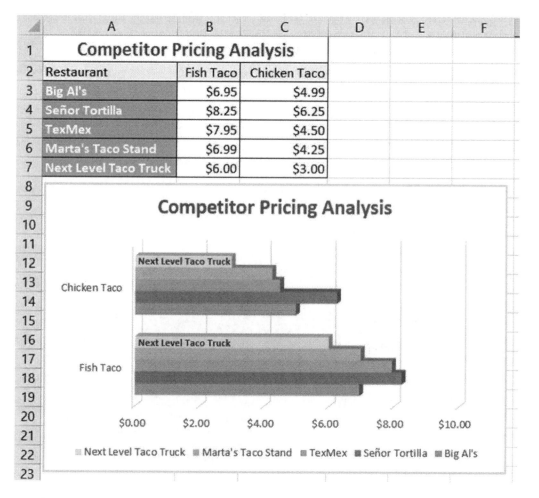

Chapter 6
Tables

Tables organize related data and provide tools for analysis.

Tables

A better way to manage related data is to create a table. Tables have sorting and filtering commands in drop-down lists and rows with alternate shading to better distinguish data. Data analysis is easier because tables use calculated columns and a totals row with drop-down lists for selecting summaries. A table is independent of the rest of the spreadsheet, and you can have multiple tables within a workbook.

To create and customize a table:

1. Select a range of related data.
2. Click Home ⇨ Format as Table. A gallery of styles is displayed.
3. Click a style (you can always change it later). A dialog box is displayed.
4. Confirm the data range for the table. Clear the My table has headers check box if you have not included a top row of labels in the data selection. Note that a header row will be added if you clear this option.
5. Click OK. The data range is formatted as a table with drop-down list arrows in the header row, similar to Figure 65.

Figure 65 A table has drop-down lists for each column.

	A	B	C
1	Date	Item	Sold
2	1/5/2017	Pretzels	23
3	1/5/2017	Chocolate	38
4	1/6/2017	Mints	16

6. *Optional*. Click in the table, if necessary, and click Table Tools Design ⇨ Total Row. A new row with totals for numeric columns is added, similar to Figure 66.

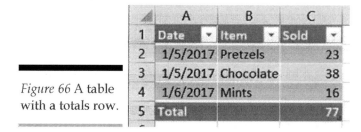

Figure 66 A table
with a totals row.

Or

With the entire table selected, click the Quick Analysis button in the lower-right corner, click Totals, and then click a totals row or column. A best guess total is added to every column or row.

7. *Optional*. Customize the totals row by clicking a cell in the row and selecting a function from the list. Figure 67 shows a totals row list.

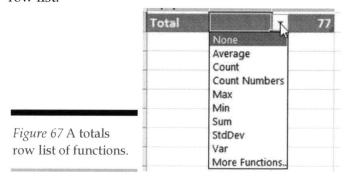

Figure 67 A totals
row list of functions.

8. *Optional*. Click the Table Tools Design tab and then customize the table using Table Tools Options and Tables Styles. Refer to Table 18.

9. *Optional*. Add a calculated column.

   a) Add a column by right-clicking an existing column and then clicking Insert and selecting the appropriate command.

   Or

   Type in the column adjacent to the last table column to add a new column to the table.

b) Select any cell in the new column and type a formula. Press Enter. The formula is copied to the entire column and cell references are changed to structured references. In Figure 68, when the formula =IF(C2>25,"Yes","No") was entered into cell D2, it was copied to the entire column and C2 was changed to a structured reference (see the Formula bar).

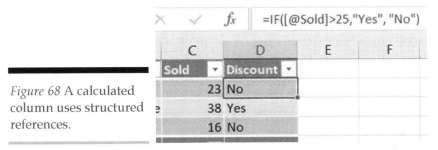

Figure 68 A calculated column uses structured references.

TIP For best results, create a table from rows of consistent data. Do not include a row with totals when you create the table. Use the Table Tools Design tab or the Quick Analysis button to add totals and summaries in a separate row or column after the table is created.

TIP You can also click Insert ⇨ Table to create a table.

TIP Right-click anywhere in a table for commands to insert or delete rows and columns.

Table 18 Table Tools Design Tab

Table Name box	Click the Table Name box and type a descriptive, defined name for the table. Prefix the name with tbl_ for good style.
Resize Table	Displays a dialog box where you can type or select a new range for the table. Alternatively, drag the sizing handle in the lower-right corner of the last table cell.
Summarize with PivotTable	Displays the Create PivotTable dialog box. Refer to "PivotTables" on pg. 91.
Remove Duplicates	Deletes duplicate rows based on the contents of the columns you select to compare.
Convert to Range	Converts the table back to a range of cells.

Insert Slicer	Create a customized filtering tool. Refer to "Slicers" on pg. 84.
External Data group	Export exports the table data to a SharePoint list or Visio diagram. Use other commands in this group if you've connected to an external data source for your table. (Use commands on the Data tab to connect to a data source.)
Table Style Options group	☑ Header Row ☐ First Column ☑ Filter Button ☑ Total Row ☐ Last Column ☑ Banded Rows ☐ Banded Columns Table Style Options Click a checkbox to add or remove an option.
Table Styles group	Click the More button in the Table Styles group for a gallery of styles. Point to a style to preview the effect. Click a style to apply it.

Sorting a Table

Sorting commands are in the drop-down list of each header in a table. (Chapter 3 discusses sorting a normal range of cells.)

To sort a table:

1. Click the arrow in the header of the column to base the sort.

2. Click Sort A to Z for ascending order.

   Or

   Click Sort Z to A for descending order.

   Or

   Click Sort by Color ⇨ Custom Sort. A dialog box is displayed.

   a) Click the arrows to select the Sort by column, the Sort On option (Values, Cell Color, Font Color, Cell Icon), and the Order.

   b) *Optional.* Click Add Level to specify a secondary sort. For example, you may want to have rows organized by Last Name and, within that sort, by First Name.

   c) Click OK to apply the sort.

Filtering a Table

When you *filter* a table, you limit the displayed rows to those which meet defined criteria. Rows that do not contain the criteria are hidden from view until you remove the filter.

To apply a quick filter to a table:

1. Click the arrow in the header of the column containing the filter criteria. The list includes a Search box, and all the data values for the column are displayed.

2. Type the filter criteria in the Search box.

   Or

   Clear and select check boxes to limit criteria to selected values.

3. Click OK. Rows that do not contain the criteria are hidden. The drop-down arrow changes to ⛛. If you hover over the button, you will see the applied criteria, as in Figure 69.

Figure 69 Hover over the filter button to see criteria.

4. To display all rows again, click ⛛ ⇨ Clear Filter.

To apply an advanced filter that shows a range of data by value:

1. Click the arrow in the header of the column containing the filter criteria. The list includes Filter commands.

2. Click a Filter command (Number Filters, Text Filters, or Date Filters). A list of comparison operators is displayed.

3. Click an operator. The Custom AutoFilter dialog box is displayed.

4. Type the criteria.

5. *Optional.* Click And or Or, select a comparison operator, and then type additional criteria to form a complex filter.

6. Click OK. Rows that do not contain the criteria are hidden.

7. To display all rows again, click ⛛ ⇨ Clear Filter.

TIP When conditional formatting or cell styles have been applied to cells in a column, the Filter by Color command is available in the drop-down list.

TIP Filtering a chart range will change what is charted.

Slicers

A *slicer* is a filtering tool that is displayed on the spreadsheet. The visual aspect of slicers make them an effective tool for interactive dashboards.

To create and use a slicer:

1. Click a cell in the table to make the table active.
2. Click Table Tools Design ⇨ Insert Slicer. A dialog box is displayed with check box options for each column in the table.
3. Click check boxes for each slicer you want to create and then select OK. Slicers are added to the spreadsheet. In Figure 70, slicers have been added for each column.

Figure 70
Slicers provide a visual filter.

4. *Optional*. Drag a slicer to position it, drag a handle on a selected slicer, if necessary, to size it, and use the Slicer Tools Options tab to customize the slicer style.
5. Click a value in a slicer to apply a filter. To create complex criteria with And, click criteria in more than one slicer. To create Or criteria involving one column, press and hold the Ctrl key while clicking multiple criteria in a single slicer.
6. Click Clear Filter in the slicer to remove the filter.

Chapter 7
Managing a Workbook

A workbook often contains multiple sheets of related data, charts, and tables. With complex workbooks, it becomes imperative to provide cell comments for better usability, protect data from unintentional changes, and collaborate with others. For further in-depth coverage of a feature, type the topic in the Tell Me box and then select the related Get Help on command.

The View Tab

The View tab Window group has options that are helpful when working with large spreadsheets and workbooks with multiple sheets:

Table 19 The View Tab Window Group

New Window	Opens another window with the same workbook so that you can work on different areas or sheets at the same time.
Arrange All	Stacks the opens windows. Along with this command, you can View Side by Side, turn on Synchronous Scrolling, and Reset Window Position.
Freeze Panes	Keeps rows and columns visible while you scroll. Select a cell just below and to the right of the rows and columns to freeze.
Split	Divides the current window into panes that can be individually scrolled. Select a cell just below and to the right of where the split is to occur. Click Split again to reverse the action.
Hide	Hides the current display. Click Unhide to reverse the action.

Cell Comments

Cell comments are notes displayed when you click a cell or hover the mouse over a cell. They are especially useful when you want to provide instructions to the user. Cells with a comment have a red indicator in the upper-right corner.

To insert and manage comments:

1. Select a cell and then click Review ⇨ New Comment. A box with a blinking insertion point is displayed.

2. Type the text for your comment and then click a different cell to close the comment box.

3. Use commands in the Comments group on the Review tab to edit, delete, and view comments.

TIP Right-click a cell for comment commands.

TIP The Review ⇨ Show Ink command applies to annotations added with a Windows tablet or pen-enabled device.

Protecting a Workbook or Worksheet

When you protect a workbook, users cannot change the structure of the file. For example, sheets cannot be hidden, deleted, or moved. On another level, a protected worksheet prevents users from changing data, formulas, and formats. However, you have the option of making ranges within a sheet accessible.

To protect a workbook and worksheet:

1. To protect the structure of a workbook, click Review ⇨ Protect Workbook. A dialog box is displayed.

2. Type a password, if desired. WARNING: A password cannot be retrieved if forgotten. Click OK. Retype the password and click OK again.

3. To protect aspects of a displayed sheet, click Review ⇨ Protect Sheet. A dialog box is displayed.

4. Type a password, if desired, and select the actions allowed by users. WARNING: A password cannot be retrieved if forgotten. Click OK. Retype the password and click OK again.

5.   *Optional*. If you want to allow users to edit a range on a protected sheet, click Review ⇨ Allow Users to Edit Ranges <u>before</u> protecting a sheet with steps 3 and 4.

    a)   Click New. Type a Title for the range, click Refers to cells. and select the range on the spreadsheet.

T I P The Review ⇨ Track Changes command keeps track of any changes made to your spreadsheet. This feature is available in shared workbooks.

Collaboration

If you want others to contribute to the development of a workbook, you will need to share it:

- Click Share in the upper-right of the spreadsheet window, save the file to Cloud, and then invite people through email to access the workbook.

- Save the workbook to a network location and then click either the Share Workbook or Protect Workbook command on the Review tab.

Note that not all workbook features are available in a shared workbook, including tables. For more information, use the Tell Me box to get help on "share a workbook".

Creating a Template

A custom template saves time when you need to create a similar workbook over and over again.

Before creating your first template:

1.   Click File ⇨ Options and then click Save.

2.   Type a location for your templates in the Default personal templates location and click OK.

To create a template:

1.   Create a spreadsheet with the titles, labels, formulas, and other unchanging data for your template.

2.   Click File ⇨ Export.

3.   Click Change File Type and then Template.

4. Click Save As below the file type list. A dialog box is displayed with Excel Template as the file type.

5. Browse to the location to store the template (if necessary), type a File Name, and click Save.

To use a template file for a new spreadsheet:

1. Click File ➪ New.

2. Above the featured templates, click Personal. Your personal template files are displayed.

3. Click a template. A new spreadsheet is created based on your template.

Macros

Repetitive tasks can be made more efficient by running a macro. A *macro* is a recording of the mouse clicks and keystrokes for performing a specific task. For example, if you regularly format a column label as bold, italic, 16 pt., you can create a macro that does this in one step rather than three.

To record a macro:

1. *Optional.* If you want the macro to run relative to the currently selected cell, then click View ➪ Macros ➪ Use Relative References. Otherwise, when a macro is run, the actions will be absolute.

2. Click View ➪ Macros ➪ Record Macro.

3. Type a descriptive name for the macro. Create a Shortcut key if desired. Complete other entries in the dialog box as needed and click OK.

4. Perform the steps for your macro, being as efficient as possible.

5. Click View ➪ Macros ➪ Stop Recording.

6. Test the macro. You run a macro by pressing the defined shortcut key or by using View ➪ Macros ➪ View Macros.

7. To save an Excel file with macros you will have to save the workbook as the file type Excel Macro-Enabled Workbook.

To assign a macro to a button on the Quick Access Toolbar:

1. Click the Quick Access Toolbar More ⌄ button and click More Commands.

    Or

    Click File ⇨ Options ⇨ Quick Access Toolbar.

2. Click Choose commands from ⇨ Macro. A list of available macros is displayed.

3. Click a macro and then click Add to move it to the Quick Access Toolbar command list.

4. *Optional*. Select the macro and click Modify. Click a symbol and then OK to assign a new button.

To manage and edit a macro:

1. Click View ⇨ Macros ⇨ View Macros and then select a macro.

2. If you want to change the shortcut, click Options.

3. If you want to see and edit the Visual Basic for Applications (VBA) code for the macro, click Edit. Close the VBA window to return to Excel.

4. Click Delete to delete the macro.

TIP Macros can sometimes be the source of malicious code. Always use a security product to scan a file you've received before opening it.

Document Inspector

The final check for a document that will be shared electronically is to remove personal information and hidden data. As helpful as it may be to wipe your document of this type data, which is referred to as *metadata*, you will also want to perform the check on a copy of your document because the metadata may not be able to be restored. The document inspector can also be used to alert you to accessibility and compatibility issues.

To remove personal information and hidden data:

1. Save your spreadsheet.

2. Click File ⇨ Save As and save your spreadsheet using a new name. (Refer to pg. 9.)

3. Click File ⇨ Info and then click Check for Issues ⇨ Inspect Document. A dialog box is displayed.

4. Read through the options and clear any content you do not want reviewed.

5. Click Inspect. A report is displayed.

6. Review the results and click Remove All where you want metadata to be deleted.

7. Click Close to remove the dialog box.

Appendix A
PivotTables, PivotCharts, and Data Models

PivotTables, PivotCharts, and Data Models demonstrate the power of an Excel spreadsheet for analyzing data. They are also the basis of interactive dashboards.

PivotTables

PivotTables are reports based on existing data. They summarize and analyze data without the need to create formulas, and multiple reports can be generated to present different views of the same data. Tables are the best source for PivotTables because updates to a table are linked to related PivotTables. PivotTables do not alter the data they are based on.

To create a PivotTable using the Recommended PivotTables command:

1. Click in the table that will be used as the PivotTable source. (PivotTables summarize when at least one column of a table contains duplicate entries.)

2. Click Insert ⇨ Recommended PivotTables. The suggested reports are based on the selected data.

3. Click a suggested PivotTable in the left pane of the dialog box for a preview.

4. With the desired PivotTable selected, click OK. A new worksheet displays the PivotTable and the PivotTable Fields pane. Although not all fields are added to every report, in general, non-numeric fields are used for rows, data/time fields are placed into columns, and numeric fields are value fields. Refer to Figure 71 as an example.

5. Refer to "Working with PivotTables" on pg. 93 to customize the report.

To manually create a PivotTable:

1.　Click in the table that will be used as the PivotTable source. (PivotTables summarize when at least one column of a table contains duplicate entries.)

2.　Click Table Tools Design ⇨ Summarize with PivotTable. A dialog box is displayed.

3.　Select a table, if necessary, choose where you want the PivotTable report, and then click OK. PivotTable instructions are displayed.

4.　In the PivotTable Fields pane, drag desired field(s) into the ROWS area. You may also optionally drag field(s) to the COLUMNS area. (You can also click a field in the fields list and Excel will make a best guess as to the area to place it.)

5.　Drag a field(s) into the VALUES area. Fields in this area generate a summary. Click the arrow ▼ next to a field in the VALUES area and click Value Field Settings for a dialog box where the summary type can be changed. Click Number Format in this dialog box to change the way the summary is displayed.

6.　Refer to "Working with PivotTables" below to customize the report.

───────────

Figure 71 The PivotTable report (right) has the Item field in the ROWS area and the Order field in the VALUES area.

◢	A	B	C	D
1	Date ▼	Cust ID ▼	Item ▼	Order ▼
2	1/3/2017	G290	Chocolate	44
3	1/3/2017	S440	Mints	14
4	1/5/2017	T954	Pretzels	32
5	1/7/2017	S440	Chocolate	23
6	1/9/2017	G290	Gum	18

Row Labels ▼	Sum of Order
Chocolate	67
Gum	18
Mints	14
Pretzels	32
Grand Total	**131**

TIP The fastest way to delete a PivotTable is to delete its sheet (right-click the sheet tab and click Delete).

TIP Another way to summarize related data is to use commands in the Outline group on the Data tab. First, sort the range based on a column with entries that can be grouped. Next, click Data ⇨ Subtotal to generate an outline with subtotals. Symbols that appear to the left of the sheet can be clicked to expand and collapse outline levels.

TIP Click Insert ⇨ PivotChart to create a PivotChart and a PivotTable in one step.

Working with PivotTables

There are endless possibilities for customizing a PivotTable report. There are also interactive features to change the data view. Below are tips to optimize, interact, and update a report (refer also to Table 20 PivotTable Tools Analyze tab):

- Click the arrow ▼ next to a field in the COLUMNS or ROWS area and click Field Settings for a dialog box where name and layout options can be changed.

- Drag any of the unused fields into the FILTERS area to add report filters above the report. You can click the arrow button in the filters to limit the rows displayed. (Refer to "Filtering a Table" on pg. 83).

- Right-click a summary and click Value Field Settings to change the format, type, or name of the summary.

- Click an arrow in the report headers for commands to apply a filter based on the data in that field. To display all data again, click ⟨🔻⟩ ⇨ Clear Filter.

- Click the PivotTable Tools Design tab for commands to customize the PivotTable design. Use options in the Layout group to change the report details. Refer to Table 21 PivotTable Tools Design tab.

- Right-click anywhere in the PivotTable and click PivotTable Options for more ways to customize the layout.

- Click PivotTable Tools Analyze ⇨ Expand Field to view related source data values for the rows. Click PivotTable Tools Analyze ⇨ Collapse Field to reverse the action. Refer to Table 20 PivotTable Tools Analyze tab for more information.

- To group PivotTable items, press and hold Ctrl while you click each item for the group. Next, right-click any selected item and click Group. Right-click the group name and click Ungroup to reverse the action.

- Add a field to the VALUES area more than once when you want multiple data analysis performed.

- Right-click data for additional commands.

- Double-click a data value to "drill down" to related data, which will be placed onto a separate spreadsheet.

- To refresh a PivotTable when related table data has changed, click PivotTable Tools Analyze ⇨ Refresh.

PivotTable Slicers and Timelines

In addition to slicers (see "Slicers", pg. 84), you can display timelines for a PivotTable that has date fields. Like slicers, timelines are an effective tool for interactive dashboards.

To create and use a timeline:

1. Click in the PivotTable to make it active.

2. Click PivotTable Tools Analyze ⇨ Insert Timeline. A dialog box is displayed with check box options for each date field.

3. Click check boxes for each timeline you want to create and then select OK.

4. *Optional.* Drag a timeline to position it, drag a handle on a selected timeline, if necessary, to size it, and use the Timeline Tools Options tab to customize the timeline style.

5. Click the time level arrow to change the level. See Figure 72.

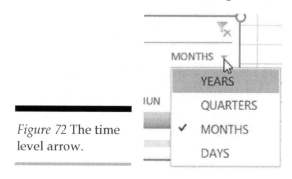

Figure 72 The time level arrow.

6. Use the scroll bar to bring time periods into view. Click in the timespan control and drag a handle (Figure 73) to change the date range.

Figure 73 Drag a timespan handle to change the range.

7. Click Clear Filter ⊽ₓ in the timeline to remove the filter.

Table 20 The PivotTable Tools Analyze Tab

PivotTable	Displays a menu. Type a defined name in the PivotTable Name box. Click Options to select format, display, and print options.
Active Field box	Type a new name for the current field.
Field Settings	Displays a dialog box of summary options.
Drill Up, Drill Down	Display a data item's children or data a level above. Applies to Data Models.
Expand Field, Collapse Field	Expand items to view related source data values. Collapse Field reverses the action.
Group Selection, Ungroup	Select rows and click Group Selection to separate data for analysis. Ungroup reverses the action.
Insert Slicer, Insert Timeline, Filter Connections	Create visual filter tools. Refer to "Slicers" on pg. 84 and "Timelines" on pg. 94. Click Filter Connections to manage filters.
Data group	Click Refresh to update a PivotTable when changes are made to the source table. Click Change Data Source to select a new source.
Actions group	Click commands in this group to Clear, Select elements, and Move PivotTable.
Fields, Items, & Sets	Displays a menu of commands to create and modify calculated fields.

Relationships	Applies to related tables. Refer to "Data Models" on pg. 97.
Tools group	Create a PivotChart or change the PivotTable.
Show group	Click commands to customize the display.

Table 21 The PivotTable Tools Design Tab

Layout group	Click a command for a menu of layout options.
PivotTable Style Options group	Click a checkbox to add or remove an option.
PivotTable Styles group	Click the More button for a gallery of styles. Point to a style to preview the effect. Click a style to apply it.

PivotCharts

PivotCharts include data series, categories, and so on, as with any chart. Additionally, PivotCharts include interactive filter controls for more powerful data analysis.

To create and customize a PivotChart:

1. Click in the PivotTable.

2. Click PivotTable Tools Analyze ⇨ PivotChart. The suggested chart types are based on the data.

3. Select a chart type and click OK. The chart is displayed and the PivotChart Fields pane is open. Note the interactive filter control(s). Figure 74 has a control above the legend. Click the arrow in the control for filter options.

Figure 74 PivotCharts have filter controls.

4. *Optional.* Click the Chart Elements button beside a selected chart to add elements, including a title, data labels, and axis title. Click the Chart Styles button to change the look of the chart.

5. *Optional.* Click the PivotChart Tools Design tab for options to change the chart style, add elements, or click Quick Layout to change the overall layout of the chart.

6. *Optional.* Click the PivotChart Tools Format tab to apply formats to objects in the chart. Select an object in the Chart Elements list and click Format Selection to open a Format pane of options.

Data Models

An Excel *Data Model* is a collection of related tables. PivotTable reports and PivotCharts are used for data visualization of the combined tables. A relationship exists between two tables when one column from a table contains unique entries that correspond to a column in a second table.

When you store data in related tables, you eliminate data redundancy and reduce errors. For example, a workbook with Orders, Customers, and Regions need only store complete customer information in one table rather than repeating it for every order made by a customer. Figure 75 shows three tables and their relationships. A PivotTable, filter control, and PivotChart combine the data into one report for the Data Model.

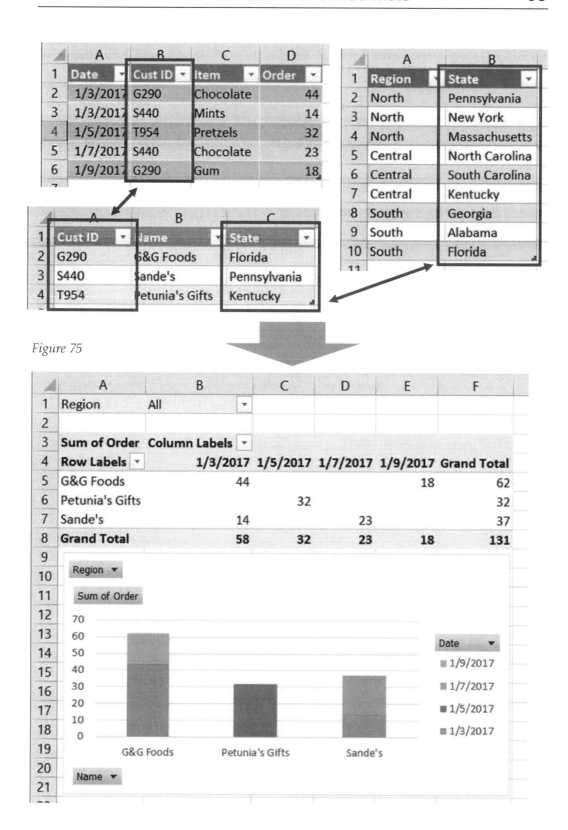

Figure 75

To create a new Data Model:

1. When creating a Data Model, it is especially helpful that each of the tables have a descriptive name (Table Tools Design ⇨ Table Name).

2. Click in one of the tables to be used in your Data Model.

3. Click Table Tools Design ⇨ Summarize with PivotTable. A dialog box is displayed.

4. The active table should already be selected. Click New Sheet, Add this data to the Data Model, and then OK. PivotTable instructions are displayed.

5. In the PivotTable Fields pane, click All. Names for all the tables in the workbook are displayed. (You are not required to use all the tables in your report.)

6. Click PivotTable Tools Analyze ⇨ Relationships. A dialog box is displayed.

7. Click New and use the New Relationship dialog box to select the Table and Related Table names and the fields they are related by. The Related Column (Primary) must contain unique entries, while the Column (Foreign) can contain duplicates that will be mapped to the primary field. Click OK to create the relationship.

8. Repeat Step 7 to define all table relationships (some tables may have multiple relationships).

9. Drag fields into the areas of the report. You may need to experiment with what works for the report, keeping in mind the table relationships.

10. If necessary, click the arrow ▼ next to a field in the VALUES area and click Value Field Settings for a dialog box where the summary type can be changed. Click Number Format in this dialog box to change the way the summary is displayed.

11. *Optional*. Add Slicers, Timelines, PivotCharts, and customize your report as outlined in the previous sections.

You can create multiple reports based on the same Data Model.

To use an existing Data Model:

1. Add a new, blank spreadsheet to the workbook and click anywhere in the sheet.

2. Click Insert ⇨ PivotTable. A dialog box is displayed.

3. Click Use this workbook's Data Model, Existing Worksheet, and then OK. PivotTable instructions are displayed. All the tables for the Data Model are displayed in the PivotTable Fields pane.

4. Drag fields into areas of the report (click the triangle next to a table to display fields). You may need to experiment with what works for the report, keeping in mind the table relationships.

5. If necessary, click the arrow ▾ next to a field in the VALUES area and click Value Field Settings for a dialog box where the summary type can be changed. Click Number Format in this dialog box to change the way the summary is displayed.

6. *Optional.* Add Slicers, Timelines, PivotCharts, and customize your report as outlined in the previous sections.

Refer to "Working with PivotTables" on pg. 93 to customize the Data Model report.

T I P Use Power Pivot for more advanced modeling. Click File ⇨ Options ⇨ Add-ins to enable this add in.

T I P Data Models and PivotTables can use external data sources, including tables from other workbooks and tables from a relational database, such as Microsoft Access. First, define an external connection with Data ⇨ Get External Data. Next, create a PivotTable and select Use an external data source and click Choose Connection.

T I P Data Model is an alternative to the VLOOKUP function.

Index

Made in the USA
Columbia, SC
11 May 2017

Conclusion

I recommend this workbook to every woman out there who wants to be practical about handling her life and takes it as what truly matters to her. To those women, who intentionally want to live above the norm by taking full control of their lives, get the best of it and be their best self.

The workbooks contain lessons, goals, action points and checklists that you can make your daily manual and help to remind you of what you really want to achieve for yourself and it will help you to lose sight of it.

62206751R00053